The Power of Indirect Influence

The Power of Indirect Influence

Judith C. Tingley, Ph.D.

AMACOM
American Management Association

New York • Atlanta • Boston • Chicago • Kansas City • San Francisco • Washington, D.C.
Brussels • Mexico City • Tokyo • Toronto

Library of Congress Cataloging-in-Publication Data

Tingley, Judith
The power of indirect influence / Judith Tingley.
    p. cm.
  ISBN 0-8144-7050-5
   1. Communication in management.   2. Communication in organizations.
3. Interpersonal communication.

HD30.3.P685   2000
658.4'5—dc21   00-045123

Printing number

10 9 8 7 6 5 4 3 2 1

Contents

Acknowledgments

Many of the ideas in *The Power of Indirect Influence* are borrowed from people whose style was always very different from mine. Jeffrey Zeig, Ph.D., introduced me to many of the concepts of indirectness, and he, in turn, was influenced earlier by Milton Erickson, M.D., a man I never knew. My appreciation of Jeff is great. He taught me, indirectly, the benefits of abandoning directness much of the time. I'm still practicing.

Thank you, too, to all the people who volunteered their stories and their experiences, anonymously or openly, despite the fact that many of them thought the topic was a little strange. Special thanks to my running buddy, Harry Wolfe, who listened endlessly to my book ideas, contributed his thoughts and examples, and tested out my suggestions in the workplace. I tried out my ideas about *The Power of Indirect Influence* in speeches to my Park Central Toastmasters group and learned a lot from their very direct and open feedback.

Appreciation goes also to Karen Killion, who helped me with the research, efficiently and intelligently; Bob Henschen, who edited the book before submission; Ellen Kadin, my editor at AMACOM, who has always been a good communicator; and Phyllis Grosscup, who has helped me in many ways with each of my four books.

Acknowledgments

I find writing a somewhat solitary activity. So I am partic-ularly appreciative of the friendship, the conversations, the interest, the experiences, and the ideas of my children, Sara, David, Steven, and Jim Dodenhoff, and my husband, Mike Killion.

The Power of Indirect Influence

Chapter 1

The Dynamic Duo

Power and Influence

etting people to do what you want or need them to do can be the most difficult task faced by leaders, managers, and CEOs. As a leader, how do you influence people successfully? Do you use the command-and-control style of communication? Do you hint around, figuring your people will get the drift and take the initiative to follow through? Do you model the behaviors you want from your employees? Do you count on the power of your position to persuade people to take action? Do you say nothing, believing that good senior managers shouldn't have to be told what to do? Do you use examples and stories as a way of inspiring people to follow your lead? Or do you try any or all of these ways to communicate so that you can be effective at influencing people, directly or indirectly?

In the business culture of the United States, the direct, assertive, or even aggressive style of communication is the preferred mode for influencing others. The direct style fits with our historic origins as a country of independent, aggressive, pioneering men and women, and with our current status as a country of entrepreneurs. Leaders are often lauded for their command-and-control style, their cut-to-the-chase communication. "She tells it like it is." "He doesn't mess around. He says exactly what he means and he gets exactly what he wants." "She leaves no doubt in your mind. You always know exactly where she is in her thinking." Those who don't speak up, who are nonassertive, are often run over by their more assertive competitors and never make it to the top.

But there is another way to communicate, verbally and nonverbally, in order to influence people: the "Beyond Assertiveness" (BA) approach. BA refers to a group of indirect influence communication techniques that are intentionally used to increase success in achieving a specific outcome. They are not "beyond" in the sense of being even more direct than assertive, but in the sense that they don't align with the continuum of nonassertive, assertive, and aggressive communication. The techniques are "beyond" assertiveness in the sense that they are in a completely different plane or sphere. They are an entirely different breed of influence skills.

Influencing people through indirect communication is an advanced skill that many U.S. managers now need to acquire. The changing emphasis on management as transformational, rather than transactional, the increasingly diverse workforce and marketplace, and the move toward transnational companies and a multinational workforce all point toward the need for a broader spectrum of influence skills.

Although direct communication is the hallmark of the Western business culture, Eastern Europe, Asia, some Western European, and many Latino cultures prefer and practice the finesse of indirect communication. In the United States there are many situations and events that also call for the subtlety, as well as the cooperative aura, of an indirect influence approach. Indirectness certainly works better with people from countries and cultures that more commonly use indirectness, and with people who are resistant to influence. But it also may work better than directness with younger employees who want to be full participants in making decisions that affect them. The more entrepreneurial, independent-contractor class of employee that's growing in size and strength often responds more favorably to an indirect rather than a direct approach. The Beyond Assertiveness approach will also work best for people who are new in a position of power, and for leaders who need not only to delegate but to inspire, to be visionaries.

Ideally, leaders have a broad range of direct and indirect communication techniques at their beck and call. Good leaders should use situational or adaptive communication in the same way they use situational leadership. They choose their style of leadership depending on the situation rather than on their personal comfort and preference. They also choose the communication approach and technique that best fits the individual or group they're attempting to influence, as well as the specific situation and context they find themselves in at any given moment. Indirect influence techniques can be a powerful part of the communication tool chest, but few leaders have learned how to use these advanced skills. They are particularly useful when: the direct approach doesn't feel right in a particular setting; the direct approach has been tried and hasn't worked; aggressive or nonassertive people are the communication recipients; or the target person or group tends to be resistant, oppositional, or defensive.

A Story

The CEO, Jim Finnegan, noticed the animosity directed at him and his company from the moment the contract was signed. Jim's company, Resources Plus, sold benefits packages to Fortune 500 companies. After two years of schmoozing, selling,

3

and negotiating, Resources Plus had finally been awarded a significant contract with an international high-tech corporation, Karbex.

At the first meeting with the Karbex human resources department, bad vibes prevailed. Jim never quite understood the origin of the apparent dislike and even hostility toward his company and his staff. He suspected the negativity may have resulted from a disagreement within the client company about which benefits vendor to use. Resources Plus had responded defensively, from the beginning, to the animosity directed at them. Their people had become reactive to criticism instead of active in pursuit of a good business relationship. No one knew how to change the pattern or alter the course of the nonrelationship.

The contract had been in effect for two problem-laden years. Nothing Jim's company did seemed to satisfy Karbex. Even he admitted that somehow more things seemed to go wrong with this particular client than with any other that Resources Plus served. Karbex's complaints escalated. A crisis was imminent. Karbex was refusing to pay the monthly fee to the service provider. The contract had only four months to go. Their head honcho was hinting that they wouldn't renew the contract, and that they also wouldn't pay for the remaining four months of the existing contract. Resources Plus made promises, suggested solutions, changed their contact people, simplified their processes, revised their written material. Nothing melted the icy climate. There were no signs of willingness to compromise on the part of the client company.

The CEO of Resources Plus was ready to surrender. Nothing he had done previously, or suggested to his staff, had altered the adversarial atmosphere. He wanted to hang on to the client, but he wasn't sure how. After considerable think time, Jim resolved to do something totally different from anything he, or Resources Plus, had ever done before. He decided to avoid the direct, competitive, somewhat defensive—even aggressive—approach that he had previously allowed and even supported. It hadn't worked! He figured that although a change in approach might come too late, he had nothing to lose.

Jim decided to attend the upcoming meeting with Karbex himself, something he had never done before. The meeting had been set up by Resources Plus to defend themselves against continuing complaints from the client organization. The traditional direct, aggressive, win-lose approach would have been to respond to each complaint and then tell Karbex if they didn't make the monthly payment, or if they didn't guarantee Resources Plus that they would renew the contract four months down the road, the CEO would withdraw from the contract himself and leave them with no service provider for the rest of the year. This type of approach would be an escalation of previous attempts to compete, defend, justify, and oppose the negativity of the client.

Jim chose, instead, to use an indirect influence approach to alter the outcome and to increase the likelihood of getting what he wanted. He decided not only to attend the meeting with his two staff members, but to redo the agenda and facilitate the meeting. Jim wanted his presence, his verbal communication, and the agenda all to deliver the same message, in indirect ways: "This business relationship is very important to me as well as to Resources Plus. It's so important that I am here to personally lend my presence, my attention, my caring, my credibility to resolving issues. I am interested in looking forward, not backward, to developing a good partnership between Karbex and Resources Plus. I want to do whatever it takes to work in a positive, problem-solving way toward gaining Karbex's comfort and satisfaction, if not delight, as our customer."

The CEO accomplished his goal without ever directly delivering the verbal message. In the past, the direct messages generally produced disbelief at best and opposition at worst.

For example, the message in the previous paragraph, delivered directly, might have been responded to by the Karbex director with sarcasm: "Sure you do." Or worse, "That's pure BS." Or perhaps, "Where have you been for the past two years? In la la land? You had plenty of chances and you blew it. Too late now."

By attending the meeting himself, facilitating the meeting, and following a new process-oriented rather than topic-oriented agenda, Jim conveyed the message he wanted to communicate, without opposition. He remained positive, upbeat, and solution-oriented as facilitator. He was pleasant, friendly, and low-key. He used active listening skills and asked a lot of questions rather than doing a lot of telling. He made no grandiose promises. He made no veiled threats. He made no open threats. He avoided discussion of past history, details of the problems, blaming, or defensiveness. He focused on the future and the benefits for both companies of developing a good working relationship. He used a variety of indirect influence techniques (all of which will be described briefly in Chapter 4).

Jim was able to pull off the change in strategy smoothly. He genuinely wanted a good working relationship with the client, and although he was frustrated with the past conflicts, he wasn't angry. He truly wanted a win-win and didn't see his ego on the line. He could afford to put himself in a one-down position for the moment, so that he had a chance to get back on an equal footing with Karbex. He believed that he and Resources Plus had to take a different tack if there was to be any route around the stormy climate that had evolved.

The indirect approach worked. Karbex withheld the monthly fee, but did guarantee renewal of the contract. Jim was able to demonstrate his interest in building trust by not demanding a contract renewal now, and not insisting on the monthly fee payment as the necessary condition to proceed. Jim celebrated the outcome. He managed to pull Resources

Plus from the shaky brink of disaster to a position of possible balance and stability. He influenced Karbex to consider changing their attitude, their belief and behavior toward his company, all accomplished with indirect influence. He was confident that if his company could decrease its errors, Karbex would stay a satisfied and long-term customer. And Jim will be using the Beyond Assertiveness approach more frequently in the future to increase the likelihood of getting what he wants as a business leader.

Getting People to Do What You Want Them to Do

Managers spend the majority of their time attempting to get people to do, or redo, or do correctly, or do better, what the manager has asked them to do. Imagine the explosion of innovation and the escalation of productivity that might emerge if a manager's first influence attempt always "took."

Everyone in a leadership position recognizes the problem of persuading people to do what you want them to do. Several years ago, at a regional conference of the National Speaker's Association, I heard Ken Blanchard speak. An audience member asked him, "Ken, when are you going to write another book and what is it going to be about?" Blanchard responded, "I'm not going to write any more books until people start doing what I've already told them to do!"

When I was making a living as a psychologist and therapist, before I became a business consultant, a good (and intelligent) friend asked, "Why does it take so long to get people feeling and doing better? Why don't you just tell your clients what they need to do in the first session, answer their questions, and then send them out to do what you told them to do? Voilà—they're fixed!"

In actuality, as a Ph.D. student in the late 1970s, I was strongly admonished never to tell clients what to do in a direct fashion because clients saw the therapist as such a powerful influence that they would immediately do what they were told. Over the years, I have laughed about that directive, because I found that clients, like customers and coworkers, rarely do what leaders tell them to do directly, even if they ask for and are paying for guidance about what they should do!

The same dilemma, getting people to do what you want them to do, exists for me as a business consultant. After I begin work with an organization, gather information and make a diagnosis, I can tell people exactly what to do. "Replace Joe with Sam." "Provide leadership training for Joe and then move him into the Team Leader job." "Start behaving more as a democratic, participative leader rather than as an authoritarian, dictatorial leader." If this direct, prescriptive approach worked, clients could save a lot of money and I could work with many more organizations. But generally, the responses to such direct advice are comments like this: "We can't do that," or "Joe can't handle that job," or "You can't teach an old dog new tricks, you know. Remember, I was in the military."

CEOs have the same problem. They may be brilliant business leaders. They may have solutions to marketing problems, production snags, and accounting dilemmas, but they can't be all things to all people, so they have to delegate. Even if they have the awareness and the time to tell the delegate exactly what to do, how and when to do it, often—and for a variety of reasons—the suggestions aren't carried out as communicated.

Similar problems are cited by Donald Meichenbaum and Dennis Turk in their book *Facilitating Treatment Adherence,* dealing with how physicians can motivate or persuade patients to do what doctors want them to do. "The efficacy of all our efforts with our patients is predicated on the assumption that they follow our proscriptions and prescriptions," write the authors, who go on to say that about half the time patients don't follow the advice or directions given them, resulting in therapeutic failure.[1]

Clearly, responsible people across the board have difficulty influencing people successfully and consistently. Many leaders stick with the simplest, and in the business culture of the United States, most accepted form of influence: telling people directly what they want them to do. "I'd like you to get this group back on track, working together as a team, rather than fighting all the time. There are a lot of challenges ahead and we have to be operating at peak performance level." Sounds fairly clear, although not necessarily complete. The delegate might have more questions: "How do you want this done?" "When do you want this done by?" "Do you want me working on it alone or with you or someone else?" Often, the leader may answer, "I don't care how you do it, but I want it done by next month. I don't want to hear about it. I don't want to talk about it. I want to show up and see the team working smoothly. I don't have time for their competitive attitude. It's interfering with productivity."

That example, in its simplest form, is a direct influence attempt, conveyed through a direct communication approach. The leader has the power by virtue of a legitimate, assigned position: senior manager, CEO, or executive VP. The target of the influence attempt is the person reporting to the leader.

Will this direct assertive approach work to achieve the desired outcome? It depends: on the influencer, the target person, and the situation. However, the single most important factor in the equation is the person making the influence attempt. In *Facilitating Treatment Adherence*, the authors speak clearly about the fact that the leader in the influence process and her approach to communication have a tremendous impact on outcome. Further, they describe a study in which patients' adherence to a treatment regime was increased by 30 percent through brief education of physicians on how to broaden their repertoire of influence skills with their patients.[2]

The same increase in effectiveness can take place in the business setting. A business leader has tremendous potential power with her team. Just as the physician is the perceived authority about treatment, the leader is perceived as the expert about her business. In both contexts, the greatest improvement in adherence to influence attempts will come from the use of a broader range of influence skills, in particular from the intentional use of indirect communication techniques.

How can the leader better use the resources in his possession to increase the probability of adherence by those influenced and thereby success? A higher rate of return on influence attempt investment can always be achieved by understanding the dynamics of power and influence, by increasing the leader's repertoire of influence strategies, and by purposefully designing the influence attempt to fit the target person or group and the specific context.

The Dynamic Duo

This dynamic duo isn't Batman and Robin. It's the duo of power and influence, the essential assets for leaders to have and use when persuading people to do what they want them to do. When used with skill and intelligence, the power and influence duo can be as strong and successful against overwhelming forces as Batman and Robin. Jim, CEO of Resources Plus, used power and influence successfully to get his client to do what he wanted them to do, without being direct, intimidating, coercive, aggressive, pushy, or difficult.

The words *power* and *influence* can both evoke a negative response, but in fact both are neutral words. *Power* as defined by the dictionary is merely the ability to do, act, or produce. *Influence* is the power of persons or things to affect others, seen only in its effects. Power is stationary. Influence is action.

You need power to influence, but power unused doesn't produce an effect.

The descriptive approach to power and influence, used in Cartwright and Zander's signal book, *Group Dynamics: Research and Theory*, is clear. They discuss the three factors that determine whether we'll achieve a desired result when we're trying to influence others: the communicator's resources of power, the responder's motive base of influence, and the method of influence used.[3]

A leader's resources of power can be as varied as skills and personality allow, but she always has legitimate power, the resource of the position itself. A title such as Director of Human Resources, or Team Leader, or COO imbues the holder of the title with some legitimate power. Generally, legitimate power alone isn't adequate to get people to do what you want them to do. Resources of power are anything that the communicator or leader has that someone else might want, need, or value: money, status, charisma, intelligence, or knowledge, for example. Resources of power can also be less tangible assets such as the ability to be funny, or a capability to cloak others with approval or affection.

The motive base of influence refers to the responder's willingness and motivation to be influenced. Possible motivating factors are the desire to be accepted, to acquire knowledge, to be promoted, or to be rewarded with money. Occasionally, people are influenced by intrinsic gratification—a certain acceptance of the desirability of change even when other motivating resources aren't present or available in the power holder.

The method of influence itself is a key factor in determining outcome. Whether you choose to hint or bully, hedge or hit hard, lighten up or get intense, how you go about influencing someone is as important as who you are, who he is, and what your relationship is. Direct methods of influence include modes of communication such as telling, ordering, commanding, requiring, persuading, rewarding, and punishing. Indirect methods of influence may be evading, acquiescing, or avoiding—the nonassertive kind of indirectness—or humor, modeling, reframing, and a whole bevy of other techniques which are the subject of this book. The decision as to whether a direct or indirect method of influence is best depends on which method is most likely to produce an outcome that matches the leader's intent.

Direct influence attempts are generally viewed as intentional attempts to influence someone. When a senior manager says, "I would like you at that Monday meeting, prepared and articulate," you know he means what he says. He is very intentionally attempting to get you to do what he wants you to do. There is no doubt about the purpose or motive. He wants you there. This is a simple statement without undertones of consequences, negative or positive. Direct influence attempts are viewed by the leader and the responder as open, honest, and intentional when they are delivered in this assertive manner. The leader's intent is to communicate in a way that the receiver can receive and understand the message, as well as act on it. The perception of this assertive communication is that the communicator is attempting to increase the probability of the responder's success.

If the same message is delivered openly, directly, honestly and intentionally—but in an aggressive manner—both the leader and the responder may view the statement as potentially punitive: "You better show up at that Monday meeting on time and know what you're talking about!" Here, the leader's intent appears to be to threaten the responder, to get her to act out of fear of negative consequences. The perception left by this aggressive communication is that the communicator is attempting to intimidate and put down the listener.

When the same message is delivered indirectly, it can take a variety of forms. If the manager says, "Are you going to be at the meeting Monday?" the employee is not certain if the purpose is to be sure he is there or if in fact the manager is just wondering. The influenced employee isn't sure if the question is a hint to be there or just a curious inquiry. This is definitely not an assertive or aggressive statement, but is it a nonassertive hint or is it an indirect influence attempt? Only the speaker knows! The difference is all in the choice and the intention of the communicator.

If the leader chooses an indirect communication technique intentionally to influence the responder, based on an assessment that indirect will work better than direct with this person, then we can say he's using indirect influence. If the leader doesn't intentionally make a choice of what to say or of what outcome he is trying to achieve with the employee, and communicates indirectly, then we can say he is being non-assertive.

Indirect influence attempts differ from direct influence attempts in a variety of ways. The most important difference, from the perspective of this book, is that indirect influence attempts are planned as intentional by the leader, but viewed as unintentional by the target person. The lack of intentionality, as perceived by the one who is influenced, is the source of strength in the influence attempt. In this book, the methods and techniques of indirect influence refer only to *intentional* indirect influence attempts.

Does indirect influence always work? Is it the best way to handle all communication situations as a leader? No. But it is an extremely useful and effective tool in the constant striving to get people to do what you want them to do. When you understand the dynamics of power and influence, the effects of authority on people's acceptance of or resistance to influence attempts, and know how and when to choose a direct or indirect method of influence, you can quickly expand your success rate in getting people to do what you want them to do.

Resistance

In contrast to direct influence attempts, indirect influence rarely engenders resistance from the target person. The concept of resistance is primary in psychotherapy, as it is in any setting or discipline where bringing about change is a goal. According to the dictionary, resistance refers to the act of resisting, opposing, or withstanding. Applied to therapy, it means the same thing, but with a slightly different spin. Traditionally, when a client resisted the therapist's message, her resistance was seen as another symptom of the client's neurosis. In more current views, client resistance is viewed as a sign of the therapist's inability to find the right way to communicate the desired message. If the therapist communicates the message skillfully, the client will be more likely to hear, accept, and perhaps even implement the suggestion.

In business, when the target person is resistant, rather than seeing this as a symptom of their problem, leaders will find that a more useful approach is to see such resistance as a sign that the communicator needs to deliver the message in a different way. The leader is the one who has the responsibility for preventing resistance, avoiding it, or breaking through it when it occurs.

Human nature being what it is, many employees, patients, customers, and clients resist the direct influence attempts made by people in positions of authority: the boss, the CEO, the physician, psychologist, or salesperson. Leaders and managers being who they are, when they experience resistance, they often try the same direct approach over and over again, expecting a different result. They don't get it. They often inadvertently generate even greater opposition.

On the other hand, indirect influence attempts, those that are perceived by the influencee as unintentional, often work quickly and easily. The "Beyond Assertiveness" approach is a group of indirect influence techniques, just as the assertiveness approach is a group of direct influence techniques. Generally, but not always, starting with indirect influence is the preferable approach. Avoid setting up the resistance, only moving to direct influence if the indirect doesn't work.

The Drill

A six-step system will help you determine whether to use a direct or indirect influence technique in specific situations with certain individuals or groups. The drill is explained in detail in Chapter 2, but here it is in brief:

- Decide what you want as an outcome of the communication.
- Read the other person in the current situation.
- Select an influencing method and technique—direct or indirect.
- Implement the technique.
- Reward yourself.
- Evaluate the results.

Another Story

Laurel, the external consultant, had concluded a one-day team-building session with the large human resources department of a major corporation. She had prepared long and hard, expending vast amounts of energy and intelligence facilitating the day-long program with thirty employees at all levels of management. Laurel felt confident that she had done an outstanding job of delivering the desired outcome.

The VP of HR, Jack, left immediately after the workshop with no comment to Laurel. The second in command of the department, Diane, said she'd call the next day to give feed-back to the facilitator. Laurel had a moment of doubt, which was substantiated the next day when Diane told her, "Every-one thought the workshop was great, useful, positive, and ex-hausting. They want you back on a quarterly basis to continue the process. Jack, however, thought you were too businesslike and professional in your style. I'm not sure if he'd agree to have you back! And as you know, he's ultimately the decision maker."

Laurel gave considerable thought to what strategy she might pursue. She wanted to continue working for this human resources department, yet she certainly didn't want to be less businesslike and professional to do so. She wished she could confront Jack directly about his comments, and Diane had given her permission to do so. If she had chosen to use an assertive, direct approach she might have said, "Jack, I spoke with Diane after the team-building workshop. I'm con-fused about your response that I was too professional and businesslike in my style. I work hard to be very professional. I'd like you to help me understand what you thought wasn't fitting about that style for that workshop." But Laurel had a sense that an assertive approach might just validate Jack's opinion that she was too businesslike and professional, char-acteristics that he clearly didn't like.

Laurel decided she would try something different. She would attempt to understand Jack's criticism of the team-building workshop and at the same time increase the likeli-hood of getting continuing work with what was essentially his department. She would do it all using an indirect rather than a direct approach, because from her information he was currently a resistant or oppositional audience. She called Jack to see if he had time for a telephone appointment with her. She said, "Getting some feedback from you about the work-shop would be extremely helpful for me, particularly in view of your knowledge and experience." Was this dishonest in view of the fact that Laurel already knew what Jack thought? No. It admittedly was not as honest or direct as telling Jack what Diane had said, and defending herself or asking for his justification, but the comment was still not dishonest.

Jack, seemingly pleased by the request, suggested they meet in person for the discussion. Laurel invited him for lunch and offered to pick him up, all to impart a slightly more friendly, social approach. At lunch Laurel was outgoing and pleasant, dressed slightly less professionally than in the navy blue business suit she'd worn at the workshop, and asked Jack many questions about himself and his background, his position, and his aspirations. Jack mentioned nothing negative about the workshop and Laurel didn't push. They had a comfortable meeting, ending with Jack's comments about working more together in the future.

When Diane called a week later, to set up a date for future work for Laurel and the human resources department, she asked, "What did you say to Jack? He's a convert! Whenever there's any problem he says, "Talk to Laurel about it," or "When Laurel comes back, we'll get her to give us some ideas.' " Laurel responded simply, "I don't know, but I'm glad both you and Jack are now feeling positive about our continuing to work together."

Just the Basics

■ The direct communication style traditionally defined the U.S. business culture but it doesn't fit the new diverse workforce, and often doesn't work for the former homogeneous workforce.

■ Leaders need to acquire and use a broad range of communication techniques to be effective.

■ Indirect influence works best when:

- The direct approach doesn't feel or seem right in a particular setting.
- The direct approach has been tried and hasn't worked.
- Aggressive or nonassertive people are the communication targets.
- The target person or group tends to be resistant, oppositional, or defensive.

■ Directly telling or asking people to do something can easily generate resistance.

■ The leader's resources of power, the target person's motive base of power, and the method of influence chosen together determine whether the influence attempt works.

Notes

1. D. Meichenbaum and D. Turk, *Facilitating Treatment Adherence* (New York: Plenum Press, 1987).
2. Ibid.
3. D. Cartwright and A. Zander, eds., *Group Dynamics: Research and Theory* (New York: Harper and Row, 1968).

Chapter 2

The Drill

 six-step framework that I call "The Drill" will help you decide when to use indirect influence communication techniques and which technique to use. The six steps are definitely a *direct* influence approach on my part. I'm proposing that you use this specific guide to become more skilled at selecting the right technique for the person and situation at hand. As soon as you recognize that you want to influence someone to do something they're not doing, you click into six-step gear and start using the system. As you gain experience and skill, the process will become intuitive. Eventually, when you've completed the influencing conversation, you'll be able to validate your thinking for each of the six steps, even though you weren't consciously thinking about the step as you proceeded.

Step 1. Deciding What You Want as an Outcome of Your Influence Attempt

A business client of mine recently asked me this question: "What should I do about the situation with Diana? She's still not doing a very good job. I don't know if I should just confront her with it, get the human resources guy to talk to her, or ask her how she thinks she's doing."

My answer to him was, "It depends on what you want as an outcome of the communication." That answer is the first question we all need to ask ourselves before any important conversation, presentation, or speech. When you know what outcome you want to achieve, you're in a much better position to choose the means to the end, the technique or approach that will be most likely to bring about the desired result.

If you have a problem with someone, a certain event or situation, your chances of having things turn out as you want are slim unless you know what you want as an outcome. This is the most important step of all. If the goal of your influence attempt is not clear in your mind at the beginning, the rest of your thinking and talking will be aimless and unproductive—and possibly disastrous.

It's like playing golf. You decide what outcome you want from your shot, and then you decide which club is the most likely means to that end. Choosing the right club isn't a guarantee that you'll make the shot, but it does increase the likelihood of achieving the outcome you want. If you're three feet from the hole, you don't choose a nine iron. If you're in a sand trap, you don't choose a driver. Communicating the same way in all situations is as futile as hitting all golf shots with a putter.

Often, we see an interpersonal communication situation as a problem. As long as we focus on the problem and don't move our thinking to the desired outcome, we're stuck. If we move to thinking about the desired outcome we want and stating it clearly, then we can start to figure out what we can or can't, will or won't, do or say to achieve the desired end. Otherwise, the interpersonal situation stays a problem ad infinitum.

Problems sound like this: "I hate to even talk to Jack. He's very defensive." Or, "Rhonda is always so negative." Or, "I don't like the way Ross is so insensitive around his female team members." Outcome statements would sound more like these: "I'd like to talk to Jack in a way that reduces his defensiveness." "I want to figure out a way to increase Rhonda's positiveness." "I'd like to help Ross better understand his female team members and treat them with more respect."

I had a business friend many years ago who always talked baby talk to me. It annoyed me. I endured the baby talk as a problem for a couple of years before turning it into a desired outcome. I wanted to scream, "Sonja, cut out the baby talk," but I realized that wouldn't work. The issue wasn't important enough for me to deal with directly, in true assertive fashion: "Sonja, I'm really uncomfortable when you talk to me as a baby would and I'd prefer you talk adult talk when we're together." She and I both would be embarrassed by such open and direct discussion of the silly topic. I ultimately chose Matching, an indirect influence technique discussed in Chapter 5, and I briefly and intermittently matched her baby talk with mine. It worked. With nothing ever said directly, she eliminated the baby talk. But, more important, in the process of changing the problem into a desired outcome I let go of a minor but nagging annoyance, and improved our relationship.

A reader of my book on direct communication, *Say What You Mean, Get What You Want*, e-mailed me a good example of how he used this first step, deciding what you want, very effectively. He had picked up the book on his way to a business trip and an important negotiation. He realized suddenly that he hadn't translated the problem he faced into a desired outcome. Cal worked in a situation in which he experienced tremendous difficulty communicating with his supervisor, Ted. Both style and professional ethics were a problem for Cal from day one with Ted. He had complained frequently about what he didn't like or want to the training manager, Joe, but up until he read *Say What You Mean,* he had not identified exactly what he did want. He finally formulated this statement: "I want to tell Joe that I would like to be reassigned to a supervisor other than Ted." When Cal clearly and concisely told Joe what he wanted, instead of what he didn't want, Joe understood quickly. Cal noted that writing out an "I want . . ." statement on the plane helped him shift his orientation from problem to solution and move more effectively to the outcome that he wanted. Until you know what you want, you can't figure out how to get it, or determine specifically what influence method and technique to use.[1]

Step 2. What's Your Read about Yourself and the Other Person in the Current Situation?

When I'm conducting workshops on communication, I like to tell a story about my friend Mary and a frog. Mary was jogging in Central Park one morning when a big green frog plopped in front of her on the jogging trail. He made loud frog noises and then said, "Pick me up and kiss me and I'll turn into a handsome prince." Well, Mary didn't give him a kiss, but she did pick him up and put him in her pocket as she kept on running. A few minutes later the frog started squirming around and getting loud again, and said, "Okay, just a hug will do and then I'll turn into a handsome prince." Mary kept on running, ignoring the restless frog. Finally, the squirming frog announced, "All right, just hold my hand, that's all I ask, and then I'll turn into a handsome prince." Mary reached into her pocket, grabbed the frog in her hand and said, "Listen, you don't understand. Handsome princes are a dime a dozen, but a talking frog, you're worth a million bucks."

What's the moral of the story? Unless you really know and understand your client, customer, manager, or coworker, you're likely to err in choosing an influence technique. The frog used a direct approach to getting what he wanted, but he made incorrect assumptions about what Mary wanted—a mistake we all make at times.

In any given influence situation, you want or need something from someone else and she in turn wants and needs something from you. You may want her to conduct a better performance appraisal of her staff, work a longer day, or improve her interpersonal skills with her coworkers. She also will want something from you—to leave her alone, to give her approval and praise, to promote her, to give her a raise, to give her a plum assignment, or to name her chair of an important committee. In deciding if there is a match, you need to determine if you have what she wants and needs and if she has what you want and need—is there a match between your resources of power and her motive base of power? If a remote possibility of a fit doesn't exist, then neither a direct nor an indirect influence attempt is going to carry much weight. If there is a possible match, you'll make a choice between a direct and an indirect approach, depending on the person and the relative power relationship.

To help understand the concept of reading the person and the situation, in action, let's look again at the example that concludes Chapter 1. The main characters are Jack, the VP of HR, and Laurel, the external consultant. She is attempting to influence him. She knows what she wants—she wants to be hired again by Jack to do more work with his company. Let's look at:

- what her resources of power are—what she has that she can use to influence Jack
- what Jack's motive base of power might be—what he might want and need from Laurel
- what else Laurel knows about him, herself, and the sit-

uation that will help her decide which mode of influence will work best—direct or indirect

When Laurel pauses to read Jack and the situation, she realizes she doesn't have much in the way of obvious resources of power. She has no legitimate power since she's external to the organization and Jack's hierarchy. She may have some expert power in the sense that Jack may think she knows more about team building than he does, but probably not. If he doesn't like her style, her expertise may be irrelevant in terms of influencing him. She doesn't have the power to punish him, but she does have the power to reward him if she can figure out what would be rewarding to him.

Step 2 is the key to advancing your communication skills and increasing the likelihood of success. You have to determine, on the basis of each specific situation, your experience and knowledge of the person, of yourself, of people, feelings, and relationships in general, and what the target person may want and need from you, before you can figure out what communication or negotiation approach to use. The range of wants or motive bases of power is endless, ranging from the mundane to the profound. People may want to be listened to, or they may want power. They may want to beat you at the game, or they may just want to avoid losing to you. They may want to avoid hard work, or they may want to replace you in your job.

Daniel Goleman calls this ability to read others "social radar," based on empathy. He also points out that a high level of self-awareness is key to understanding others' emotional landscape. If you aren't tuned in to yourself, recognizing your own internal cognitive and emotional dynamics, tuning in to others accurately is almost impossible. You don't have any internal database of knowledge for comparison, or a process of introspection that you can apply to "extrospection." Without self-awareness, you may not be good at putting yourself in the other person's shoes, never mind his head, heart, or soul. If you already have it, great. If not, try therapy, or a personality assessment and a training program at your place of business, or a course at your local community college—perhaps you perceive these moves as painful, even embarrassing, but they are essential if you want to be an advanced influencer.[2]

You can beef up your knowledge and skill in the arena of social radar by talking to people more often, listening attentively, focusing on their unspoken as well as their spoken thoughts and feelings, and then attempting to validate your perceptions by using active listening skills. "You seem stressed about the politics at work," or "Sounds like you're concerned about getting the project you want." Reading about people, feelings, and relationships can also help boost your ability to empathize. Books such as Daniel Goleman's *Emotional Intelligence*, Robert Bramson's *Coping with Difficult People*, my own *Genderflex™: Men and Women Speaking Each Other's Language at Work*, or biographies and autobiographies that delve into the inner lives of people are all possible vehicles for broadening your ability to read yourself and others more effectively.

Take a minute now as you're reading and think of a person and a situation where you want to make an impact—you want to influence someone. Jot down on the following worksheet what you want from whom. (You can check Appendix A to see a model, using Jack and Laurel.) Then write down what resource of power you have as well as what motive base of power he may have. In other words, what do you have that you can use to influence him? And what do you read in him about what he wants and needs from you? Is there a near fit or a possible match? Do you have what he appears to want or need? If not, can you figure out how to make a match?

Next, look at and write down some characteristics that you know from past experience about yourself, and the target person, that might contribute to your decision about whether

---

Worksheet 1

1. What do I want, from whom?

   _____

2. What resources of power do I have?

   _____

3. What motive base of power does he have? What does he want from me?

   _____

4. Is there a potential match or fit?

   _____

5. What characteristics do I know about him that are relevant to this influence situation?

   _____

6. What characteristics do I know about him that are particularly important in this influence situation?

   _____

---

to ultimately use a direct or indirect approach. Is the other person usually difficult, resistant, negative, or oppositional? Are you more comfortable or more skilled with a direct or indirect style of influence? Is he a direct communicator himself? Is he more similar to you, or more different in terms of personality? How can you deliver what he wants and needs in a way that he can receive it? And finally, can you do all of this without selling your soul? You don't need to answer each one of these questions. They're a sample of some of the kinds of information you might want to know before you select an influencing technique.

In addition to reading yourself and the other person, recognizing some characteristics of the situation is important: time, priority or importance of the potential influence outcome, and availability of opportunities for influence. If this is an emergency, you probably don't have time for an indirect approach unless you're very experienced, know the person extremely well, and have a bundle of communication techniques at your disposal. Indirect influence generally takes more times, over time, than a direct approach. When you're working at influencing someone very quickly, a direct communication technique may be necessary, even if you have less power or she is resistant. According to the tenets of situational leadership, when there's a fire, or similar emergency events, an autocratic approach is best. Shouting "Fire," followed by "Everyone exit through the back door," is certainly better than "Let's get consensus here. What will work best in this fire situation?" On the other hand, when you're deciding on timelines for a team project, or how to solve a nonurgent problem, a democratic approach works best.

Sometimes, you can bring about immediate change with one "Acting in Accord" or one "Reframing" indirect influence technique. Generally, the time frame that works best for indirectness is more time, to use different techniques, over time, and produce a gradual impact. Fons Trompenaars, author of *Riding the Waves of Culture*, suggests that you will always save time by using the method of influence that best fits the person, the situation, and the culture.[3]

If a situation is life and death, meaning it's critical that you accomplish the influence attempt, then you must plan in advance and make the time and opportunities available. For example, if you want to fire someone on your staff because he is actually harmful to customer relationships, but he is an employee with a good long-term work record up until he came to work for you a year ago, you will have to make the influence attempts work. The situation calls for a variety of different kinds of influence techniques and approaches, used in conjunction with several people, singly and in a group.

Finally, looking at the opportunities for influencing is another aspect of reading the situation. That means recognizing not just the time, but the vehicles available for influence: in person, in a group, by e-mail, voice mail, memo, letter, fax, all of the above, or none of the above. This choice requires knowledge of what's available in the environment, but also of what works best for you and what appears to work best for the target of the influence attempt. Yes, you do have to be a mind reader and an environmental scanner to accomplish Step 2.

Are you now somewhat confused about time and priority as factors in choosing whether the desired influence approach should be directness or indirectness? I hope so. In the last three paragraphs I was attempting to use "The Confusing Technique," which you'll read more about in Chapter 9. My goal? To have you be so confused by my explanation that you give up on me and come up with some ideas of your own about the timing and priority factors as they relate to choosing an indirect or direct approach to influence. If you find other parts of the text that are confusing to you, it will be my fault because this is the only place where I planned to be confusing.

When you're attempting to influence someone, you need

to marshal all the information you have in hand to make your influence attempt adaptive to that person and that situation, but the least important piece of information to analyze is your comfort in talking, and your determination to talk, in the way you want to. Step 2 is not the place to say, "Well, I'm just a straight-shooter kind of person and I always have been. I don't want to change. That would be phony." Or, "I'm not comfortable enough or confident enough to be direct in this situation, even though maybe I should be." Or, "These indirect techniques seem manipulative. I just can't do it." This is the time to bring out all your adaptive communication talents, to be flexible, open, creative, and versatile, to take some small risks, to try out some new behaviors, to learn some more advanced skills by practicing what's not comfortable for you.

Suzette Elgin, in her book *The Last Word on the Gentle Art of Verbal Self-Defense*, says: "In every language interaction, the adjustments you make in your language behavior should always be . . . based on the information you get from your listener's reaction to what you say. There are few communication strategies more guaranteed to fail than making adjustments based upon nothing but your personal determination to talk in a particular way *no matter what happens*."[4] When you're lifting a glass, or a rock, you adapt your grip and your muscle to the object and the situation. When you're looking far away, or nearby, you adapt your eyes and your vision to the object and the situation. Certainly, when you're attempting to influence someone, you also adapt your communication technique to the object and the situation.

Step 3. Pick the Method and the Technique

Now take all that data you just collected about everyone and everything, and put it together with what you know about which influence approach works best under given circumstances. Assertiveness is not always the communication approach of choice. Just as with situational leadership—an approach that suggests the type of leadership approach should be based on the situation, the task, and the level of the followers—there is situational communication. It's important to understand when to use the direct approach, as well as how to use the direct approach. Alberti and Emmons, in *Your Perfect Right*, identify certain kinds of people, or types of situations, where the direct approach doesn't fit:[5]

- with an overly sensitive person who is threatened by even slight disagreement or conflict
- with a very aggressive or bullying kind of person
- with an oppositional person
- with someone who is already resistant to your ideas
- when the person seems to have recognized they've taken advantage of you, and changed their behavior even if they don't necessarily apologize or acknowledge their behavior
- when you can tell that the person is having a difficult time, or a bad day, and you choose to let whatever happened go or postpone a confrontation.

Here are some clear indications for using open, honest, and direct techniques:

- People tell you that you need to be more direct.
- People tell you that you need to be more specific.
- People tell you that you need to be more concise.
- People tell you that you need to get to the point.
- People tell you that they can't read your mind; they ask you to tell them what's on your mind.
- Many people don't seem to understand you.

- People are afraid of you or are intimidated by you.
- You often feel like a doormat.
- You often feel unappreciated.
- People don't do what you want them to do.
- "Unfinished business" with people whirls around in your mind—sometimes for days after a conversation has concluded.
- You've tried hinting, suggesting, wishing, telling someone else, hoping they'd tell the target person—and it hasn't accomplished what you'd like. Nothing happens.

Or when:

- The other person is direct and assertive.
- The receiver is relatively open and nondefensive.
- The other person is confident and not intimidated by you.
- You as the speaker have strong resources of power.
- You have no hidden agenda.
- You as the speaker are not broadly skilled as a communicator and not needy.
- There's a good fit between your resources and the receiver's motive base of power.

Indirect influence techniques are the best way to influence people in a myriad of situations. There are many interpersonal dynamics which dictate that some people will be much more willing to do what you want them to do if they don't know consciously what you want them to do—or even that you want them to do something. Here are some of the situations in which the indirect approach fits well:

- People tell you that you're too blunt.
- People are afraid of you or are intimidated by you.
- People don't do what you tell them to do when you tell them directly.
- "Unfinished business" with people whirls around in your mind—sometimes for days after a conversation has concluded.
- The target person is an aggressive or nonassertive communicator.
- You've thought through or tried the direct approach and decided it won't work.
- The target person is oppositional, the kind of person who says "black" if you say "white."
- The target person tends to be hostile, defensive, or resistant.
- You know the target person feels that he has to win.

Or when:

- You as the speaker have a weak resource of power.
- You have a hidden agenda.
- You're skilled and not needy.
- There isn't a good fit between your resources and the receiver's motive base of power.

If you use a direct approach, and it doesn't fit or doesn't work, coming back with an indirect approach is often ineffective because you've already elevated the reactivity of the target person, whether it's increased sensitivity or increased opposition to you. There's rarely a time when an indirect approach doesn't fit, except in an emergency. There may be situations and people with whom it doesn't work, but using indirect influence first won't prevent you from using direct influence later. Generally, a failed indirect influence attempt doesn't result in increased resistance or resentment as a failed direct approach can.

Here's what happened with Laurel and Jack. After giving the situation considerable thought, Laurel began to understand that Jack thought quite highly of himself and had a need for acknowledgment and recognition from others—in this case from her in particular, and in front of his group. She realized that his comment that she was too businesslike and professional perhaps reflected the fact that she had treated him the same as she did every other member of the team, and did not pick him out for special treatment in any way, including not sitting with him at lunch. She decided that if she now gave him what she concluded he wanted from her, she had a shot at getting what she wanted from him. She also knew herself well enough to know she could take a "strong one-down position" without feeling less-than in this situation. And she knew she had a broad repertoire of communication techniques that she could use. But an indirect approach was called for with Jack in this situation because:

- He was male and she was female.
- Laurel had less legitimate power than Jack.
- Jack was somewhat resistant to Laurel.
- The direct approach would be viewed by Jack as "too professional and businesslike," qualities he already said he didn't like in Laurel.
- There wasn't an immediate good fit between what Laurel wanted from Jack and what Jack wanted from Laurel.

There was no rush in this situation. Though it was important, it wasn't urgent, and there would be several possible opportunities to connect since she and Jack lived in the same city. Laurel decided to take it slowly. Also, because of the specifics of the situation, she decided that a telephone meeting or a somewhat social get-together, such as a business lunch, would work better than a face-to-face meeting at Jack's office.

Laurel used indirect influence, specifically employing the technique of "Acting in Accord," (Chapter 6) to give Jack what she thought he wanted and needed from her—a more friendly, personal, social approach. She also used "Reframing," (Chapter 7) painting him as the expert rather than herself. It worked.

Just as sales professionals need to truly understand their customer to succeed, managers have to really understand their target person in order to choose the right method of influence and the right communication technique. Some of the specific direct techniques are described in the next chapter, and you'll find more in *Say What You Mean, Get What You Want*. The indirect method and its techniques are the topic of Chapters 4 through 12.

Step 4. Implement the Technique

Once you've figured out what method of influence and what technique to use, plan for when, where, and what medium you're going to use—face-to-face, e-mail, voice mail, phone, fax, public, or private. Perhaps you'll use more than one medium. If you're not sure, or find yourself hesitant to carry out your plan, rethink it briefly, but then talk it over with someone you trust, preferably someone who's similar to the target person, and ask for their feedback. The important point is to carry out your plan. Particularly when you're contemplating a technique that you're inexperienced with, you may be reluctant to act because it's new behavior and unfamiliar. One advantage of this approach is that you risk less than you would with an aggressive, or even a direct approach. Conceivably you may also gain less, but you still are usually not left in an awkward, embarrassing, one-down position if indirectness doesn't fit or doesn't work. You can always try another indirect technique, or review the steps and decide if maybe you want to try directness for the second round.

Step 5. Reward Yourself

Whether your technique worked or didn't work, give yourself a pat on the back, a movie, a nap, an hour of staring into space, a hot fudge sundae, a margarita and nachos, or whatever will feel rewarding to you—your own reward for the effort of planning and carrying out the technique. If you reward yourself only when a specific approach or technique works, you'll be less likely to take a risk, try something new, or be adventuresome in your influence attempts. The reinforcement should be simply for doing it, not for doing it brilliantly and successfully.

Step 6. Evaluate the Results

After you've rewarded yourself for attempting an influence technique, it's time to look back at all the steps and see what data was crucial in determining your success or lack of success. Did you decide what you wanted as an outcome? Did you read the person wrong? Or yourself? Was the approach or the technique not quite right? Or was everything right on except for your actual implementation? Did you not do a good job of using the technique you chose? Did you mix an indirect approach with a direct one? Had something changed between your formulation and implementation that changed the outcome? Review the data and decisions, then leave it behind if you were successful, or if you weren't, start at the beginning again with the "I want" statement. Once you become more experienced with this approach, you'll be able to glide smoothly through the steps without a conscious thought.

Stay in Step

- Remember the framework.
  - Decide what you want as an outcome of the communication.
  - Read the other person in the current situation.
  - Select an influencing method and technique—direct or indirect.
  - Implement the technique.
  - Reward yourself.
  - Evaluate the results.

- Knowing what you want as a result of your conversation is a necessity for any kind of good communication.

- Skills at reading yourself and the other person in the specific communication situation are essential for choosing the right method of influence—particularly when you're considering the indirect techniques.

Notes

1. See J. Tingley, *Say What You Mean, Get What You Want* (New York: AMACOM, 1996).
2. See D. Goleman, *Emotional Intelligence* (New York: Bantam Books, 1997).

3. F. Trompenaars, *Riding the Waves of Culture* (London: The Economist Books Ltd., 1993).
4. S. Elgin, *The Last Word on the Gentle Art of Verbal Self-Defense* (New York: Prentice Hall, 1987).
5. R. Alberti and M. Emmons, *Your Perfect Right: A Guide to Assertive Living,* 7th ed. (San Luis Obispo, Ca.: Impact Publishers, 1995).

Chapter 3

Direct Influence

The Traditional Coin of the Realm

Ferdinand F. Fournies wrote a wonderful and practical book for leaders, *Why Employees Don't Do What They're Supposed to Do: And What to Do about It*. He starts out with some potent criticism of psychologists for their inadequate contribution to the understanding of motivation. When you ask why people don't do the work they're supposed to do, psychologists respond, "Because they're not motivated." When you ask, "Why aren't they motivated?" you hear, "Because they don't want to do it." When the next question follows, "Why don't they want to do it?" you get the answer, "They aren't motivated." Fournies is appalled at this circular, useless reasoning. Instead he cites specific reasons that employees don't do what they're supposed to do, based on his research: They don't know what they're supposed to do, they don't know how to do it, they think their way is better, plus many more. He says all blame for problems and much credit for solutions should go to the manager, whose responsibility it is to take action so employees will do what they're supposed to do. His ideas are great. They're specific and concrete. They probably work under many circumstances, and they all involve the use of direct influence techniques.[1]

We all know what direct verbal influence implies—an unadorned, straightforward, candid question or statement asking or telling someone what you want her to do, what you want to do, or what you will or won't do. "I'd like you to stay late tonight and finish this project." "I'm not willing to do that, but I will come in early tomorrow morning and have it on your desk by eight A.M." Or, "Will you tell me when you're ready to present your findings to the committee?" which is really just another way to say, "Tell me when . . ."

Studies of the perceived value of direct and indirect influence strategies consistently demonstrate that direct communication strategies are assigned greater value than indirect strategies by both women and men. Directness is the first choice of both. Indirect approaches are viewed as strategies of last resort.

Specifically, a cross-cultural comparison of the U.S. culture with Japanese and Korean cultures, which was more focused on personal than business relationships, concluded that the Western preference for direct versus indirect strategies is robust and generalizable to other cultures. The authors, Steil and Hillman, found high choice for techniques of stating importance, convincing, and reasoning, and last-resort choice for techniques to acquiesce, evade, or use an advocate. This preference was consistent regardless of cultural group, participant sex, target sex, or target authority.[2]

Direct verbal communication is an open, honest expression of feelings, with or without a specific want: "I feel very annoyed when you ask me to work overtime three nights a week." You may expect to influence your boss by letting him know your feelings—the effects of his actions on you. Without a directly stated want, he may not understand what you want. You could add your wants to be more influential: "And I'd like to only work one night a week overtime." You are using a direct verbal communication approach to influence someone, to get them to do, or not do, something that you want them to do, or not do. It may be simply that you want them to understand your viewpoint, or the effect on you of their actions. But perhaps you want them to respond in a more active way—for example, by asking you to stay late less often.

Direct communication, referred to as "assertive communication" by Joseph Wolpe in 1966, was first proposed as a therapeutic approach to gain confidence and improve communication skills. Direct communication came to the forefront of popular consciousness in 1970, when Robert Alberti and Michael Emmons published their pioneering book, *Your Perfect Right*: *A Guide to Assertive Living.* The book is now in its seventh edition and has sold more than a million copies. The ideas it expresses are no longer new to most men and women in business, but thirty years ago, they were quite surprising and dramatic. Readers weren't quite sure what the authors were advocating. Were Alberti and Emmons actually saying you should tell people what you want instead of hinting around? Did the authors really believe that saying a direct "no" to a request, because you just didn't want to do something, was going to be okay? Were they overturning all rules of politeness and suggesting that everyone start to be just plain rude to one another in their personal and work life?

The authors didn't and don't see assertiveness as unacceptable, rude, crude, or brutally honest, of course. They tell us that they advocate *equality* as a communication style. "Not 'getting your way.' Not 'getting back' at the other person. And not 'turning the other cheek.' . . . Assertive behavior promotes equality in human relationships, enabling us to act in our own best interest, to stand up for ourselves without undue anxiety, to express feelings honestly and comfortably, to exercise personal rights without denying the rights of others," Alberti and Emmons said by way of definition.[3]

They, and other authors on the subject, put forth comparative definitions of three types of communication: assertive, nonassertive, and aggressive. While assertive behavior is characterized by active, direct, and honest communication, a win-win approach that works by influencing others to choose to cooperate willingly, nonassertiveness is viewed as passive and indirect. Nonassertive behavior leads to a win-lose situation where the nonassertive person becomes a loser, a victim, not a winner. In contrast, aggressiveness can be either direct or indirect communication, but underlying the influence attempt is a move to deny others their rights or choices. It's win-lose again, but this time it's the speaker who wins, and the object of the influence attempt who loses.

Men and Women

Years before Wolpe wrote about assertiveness, the accepted American mode consisted of straightforward, tell-it-like-it-is, plain-talk, bottom-line communication—perhaps emanating from the explorers and pioneers of the West and carried forth by cowboy tradition, or perhaps by the early settlers of the East, mostly men making many tough decisions in a rugged and hostile environment. "Shooting from the hip" is an expression that is used more often today to describe a style of talking than a style of shooting—at least in business. And it is a way of describing men's communication style, generally, rather than women's. Men's style has tended to consist of brief, specific, get-to-the-point comments. Men are known for telling, rather than listening, for ordering rather than asking, for occasionally being impolite and brutally honest. There's little "eggshell walking," excessive words or detail, or "softening" of the message—at least when men talk to men.

In management, as in the military, or in sports and selling, the direct and even pushy approach, the command-and-control tactic, the quick decision and expected quick response, is the modus operandi. Whether necessity is the mother of the direct communication invention for men or has always been in the genes is unclear. But most people would agree that most men continue to be more direct than most women—at least when they're talking about traditionally "male" topics such as business, money, and sports, and when they're talking to other men.

Women, for many reasons also having to do with history, socialization, genes, and stereotyping, developed a less direct approach, a more nonassertive stance over the years. They used many forms of communication that traditionally were viewed as less powerful than the direct style of men. They asked more than they told. "Isn't it a lovely day today?" They were polite and genteel, apologizing and pleasing others, rather than confronting and challenging. They used more details, more adjectives and adverbs, to describe events or people. "That darling little newsletter she sends out is really just so much fun." They told stories and recited poems to make a point. Women often hinted rather than asked for what they wanted. "Would there be any usefulness in my going to the meeting today since you can't attend?" Read a Jane Austen novel to hear the nonassertive female style at its peak. You can also find great examples of manipulative indirect influence as opposed to win-win indirect influence (the "Beyond Assertiveness" approach) in Victorian novels.

Not surprisingly, women, steeped in the tradition of nonassertiveness, were the most prevalent attendees of the early assertiveness classes. They were striving to learn the more accepted speaking style of men so that they could succeed in business, just as they were wearing navy blue power suits and bow ties to achieve the same desired outcome. They thought that looking like men, talking like men, and acting like men were key to their success. And for many years in the 1970s and early 1980s, women continued to think that the more like men they could seem, the better were their chances for success in the corporate culture.

Unfortunately, women who were very direct and attempted the conversational domination previously associated with men were labeled "bitches" or "dykes," often by women as well as by men. But the nonassertive approach certainly didn't work for women either. Natasha Josefowitz wrote a great poem, in her book *Paths to Power*, describing the no-win situation of women in the workforce of the early 1980s.[4]

Good Management Potential

If I'm assertive
I'm seen as aggressive,
If I'm aggressive I'm a bitch—
I won't be promoted.

Let's try it again:
If I'm non-assertive
I'm seen as a patsy,
If I'm a patsy
I won't be promoted.

Let's try it once more:
If I'm very careful
I can go unnoticed;
If I'm unnoticed,
No one will know
I want to be
promoted.
Any suggestions?

Many women ended the twentieth century with some of the same ambivalence about their communication style as they had when they entered the workplace of the 1980s, even though times had certainly changed. But men still dominate the power positions in organizations. Should women or should they not be direct and take the flak that goes with it? Should they instead soften their approach in order to avoid being labeled or excluded? Perhaps bouncing back and forth between extremes of directness and passivity and politeness would work best? As women continue to be more different from men, and from each other, than men are from each other, they are individually finding the styles that work best for them. As a group, women are often more adaptive than men, because they've had to adapt to thrive in what has been a male-dominated world. They are generally more skillful than men in analyzing the situation, and making a planned choice—the direct or indirect style of influence.

Cultural Difference

Generally, the concept of direct or assertive communication is accepted, supported, and practiced in Western cultures. Yet there are still people in the United States who think direct communication lacks finesse, is brutal in its honesty, or is rude, offensive, impolite, and pushy. For the most part, these critics are not those in the business culture; they tend to be people who are themselves nonassertive, or women who are less comfortable with using or hearing assertive communication. But the traditional male approach of assertiveness or even aggressiveness is still the accepted way at work in the United States.

However, in some European countries, many Asian countries, and many parts of Central and South America, direct communication is avoided like the plague in order to eliminate the possibility of confrontation, offense, or the appearance of rudeness in personal and business relationships.

In his book *Riding the Waves of Culture*, Frons Trompenaars talks about dimensions of difference between cultures. He says that the dimensions of specificity and diffuseness in communication are strategies for getting to know other people. The specific-diffuse continuum best fits, although not totally accurately, the direct-indirect influence continuum.

He notes some characteristics of specificity:

- Direct, to the point, and purposeful in relating.
- Precise, blunt, definitive, and transparent.
- Confrontational, but not personal.
- Clear, precise, and detailed instructions assure compliance or allow dissent in clear terms.

Characteristics of diffuseness are:

- Indirect, circuitous, seemingly "aimless" forms of relating.
- Evasive, tactful, ambiguous, even opaque communication.
- Patience and respect for others' ways of being and talking.
- Ambiguous, vague instructions are seen as allowing interpretations through which employees can exercise personal judgment.

Trompenaars creates a continuum by country, situating the United States, Northern Europe, and Scandinavia at the specific or direct influence end and Asia and East Africa at the diffuse or indirect influence end. His perspective is interesting and unusual.[5]

Certainly, an abundance of business books continue to underscore the importance of direct communication in the business world of the United States. Across the board, research findings demonstrate that here, direct influence strategies are viewed as more valuable than indirect strategies.

My own 1996 book, *Say What You Mean, Get What You Want,* stresses the importance of mastering a direct communication style in the workplace of the next century. Directness is certainly not the only or the best style for communicating in all situations, but it is an essential skill in the increasingly broad repertoire of communication skills demanded of us all in our work. Time and time again, research in sales, in management, in manufacturing, and about teamwork reveals that communication problems continue to be the number-one challenge for people working together. Unless you know how to communicate directly, and know that you can carry directness off successfully most of the time, you often don't have the confidence, never mind the competence, to expand into the broad and innovative array of indirect influence skills that you'll need in the continually diversifying workplace. Directness is the foundation, the infrastructure, for all other advanced influence skills.

Direct Influence Techniques

The first step for many people in preparing to use direct communication is to get rid of the negative thinking that invades their brains and sometimes prevents them from acting. "I'll hurt his feelings." "He won't like me anymore." "She'll just retaliate." "I can't deal with confrontation." "I can't stand conflict." "I want to avoid a challenging situation." "He'll get ticked off and then blow up and I won't know what to do." Eliminating this kind of thinking is essential to success in making any kind of purposeful influence attempt. Once you're thinking neutrally rather than negatively, your fear of consequences decreases and you're confident enough to use the appropriate techniques.

There are a variety of ways to alter your negative thinking patterns, but one of the most useful is *cognitive restructuring*. In plain terms, that phrase means to change what you're saying to yourself. You don't need to change the thinking to positive thinking, but to good neutral instructions. For example, instead of changing "I'll hurt his feelings," a negative thought that will get in your way, to "He'll be glad to receive this criticism," a positive thought, but probably not accurate, you might just give yourself clear, neutral instructions. For example, "My job includes giving people feedback to help them do a better job." When you make this kind of change in your internal dialogue, you'll move forward more quickly and easily with your direct influence attempt.

Saying "No"

Although any number of combinations and permutations of words and sentences could be considered direct and assertive, I've described ten specific approaches in *Say What You Mean, Get What You Want*. I write in detail first about saying "no" directly because, until you become skilled enough or brave enough to say "no" as an initiator or a responder, you probably can't be confident enough to deal with criticism, to risk rejection, or to tell people what you want.

The technique itself is simple. When someone asks you to do something you don't want to do, and don't have to do, you simply say "no" followed by one short sentence of explanation—not an excuse or an apology, just a reason. For example, you could say "No, Ellen. I don't want to go to the movies this afternoon," or "No, staying late tonight just won't work for me." The important piece is to say "no" immediately so no one is the least bit confused about what you mean. When the speaker rambles on and says, "I'd really love to go to the movies this afternoon, Ellen. You know how much I've wanted to see that particular movie. Meryl Streep is always so fabulous. But I just have some things I should do. My house is a mess and I have a project due at work. You know how it goes," the listener isn't quite sure if the answer is "yes" or "no."

If making a brief statement seems too tough, you can always add a softener for your own comfort. "No, I'm not able to chair another committee at this time. Try me again after the third quarter if you still need someone." You can also soften the "no" by being the initiator of the action. For example, in the situation just cited, you might say before being asked, "Karen, I just wanted to let you know that I'm not available to take on any more committee work this quarter." That's a good approach if you're concerned about your ability to say "no" as a response, or if you're overly, or even realistically, concerned that the other person will feel rejected, abandoned, or angry.

Making "I" Statements

The next most important technique is just using "I" statements, rather than general comments or "you" statements. Here's the difference:

- "I'd prefer to start the meeting at eight A.M." An "I" statement.
- "Early meetings usually work well for us. Eight A.M.?" A general statement.
- "You guys like to start early usually. What about eight A.M.?" A "you" statement.

The point is to tell people clearly what you want, in situations that are important to you, so they don't have to guess or read your mind. Saying what you want doesn't guarantee that you'll get it, but it does at least increase the likelihood and places you in a clearer negotiating position. There's nothing wrong with the general or the "you" statement, except that it's less clear and direct. If you're choosing to be direct, use "I" at the beginning of the sentence followed by "want," "prefer," "would like," or other expressions of preference followed by the outcome you want. People will understand and respond.

Be Brief and Specific

Direct communication is concise. The shorter the message, the greater the chance that the target person will "get it," barring some hidden agenda or underlying conflict. Cut to the chase, get to the point, say what you mean briefly and specifically—that's the way to go if you're trying to be direct. Generally, the listener doesn't need to know the history of the project, the problems you've had, or the barriers you've had to overcome that have caused you to miss the deadline. She just wants to know "when." If she wants to know "why," she can ask.

The more words and phrases, the more adverbs and adjectives, the more softeners, disclaimers, and apologies verbalized, the more circuitous the message. "I'll finish the project two days later than originally planned" is clear. "I really feel bad, but somehow or other things have slipped away and I'm not sure we can reach the targeted deadline for the project. There's still a possibility I guess, and I'd like to finish on time, but it's looking kind of iffy" is vague.

Make Statements, Don't Ask Questions

What's the problem with asking questions? Nothing, as long as you're not trying to avoid stating what you want, need, or are experiencing by putting your thoughts or feelings on the other person. For example, when you ask, "Do you think it would be best to have the company picnic on Sunday?" because you don't want to say, "I think Sunday would be the best day to have the company picnic," then you're not being direct. If you truly want information and aren't using the question as a "disguise," then asking is certainly okay. "How many people would prefer Saturday and how many people would prefer Sunday for the company picnic?" is an information-gathering question.

In general, statements come across as more assertive and powerful than questions, unless you're into interrogation, which may sound aggressive and hostile. Questions such as, "Why didn't you call me first before you made that decision?" or "What were you thinking of?" or "How could you possibly have come to that conclusion?" seem intimidating. In particular, the "why" question puts just about anyone on the defensive, even if the speaker doesn't intend to do so. The defensiveness goes back to childhood, when our parents asked us "why" our room was such a mess rather than "why" we made such good grades. Again, a statement ascertaining the information you want would be more direct and clear, and less potentially frightening: "I'd like to understand what your thinking was about opening the new plant in November instead of December." In contrast, saying "Why did you decide to open the new plant in November instead of December?" can come across as critical instead of information seeking.

Broken Record

No secret here! "Broken record" means just what you think it means. Of course, today's teens may not even know what a record is, so they would have trouble understanding the result of a broken one, going around and around, repeating the same sound over and over. But in the lingo of assertiveness, the broken record technique means to repeat your message, perhaps in slightly different ways, in order to get your point across directly, particularly in the face of conflict. For example, you're talking to your business partner and say, "I think the marketing materials are something we should share expenses equally on, although I think the cost of the office space itself should be prorated in some manner since I clearly have the larger space." Your partner responds, "The marketing materials should be prorated, too. You'll generate more revenue from them than I will so I shouldn't have to pay half of their cost." You just continue to make comments, regardless of his or her counter. "I think splitting the cost is best." "The marketing materials are best a shared expense." "We need to be equally invested in marketing the company." Being brief and specific with your broken record helps avoid going off on tangents, losing your cool, and getting pulled off course. It may or may not work to get what you want, but at least the broken record is direct and increases the likelihood of staying on target. It also keeps the other person from making inroads on your strongly stated position.

Telling What You Want

Telling what you want is an elaboration of an "I" statement. The technique encompasses three segments: *I feel . . . when you . . . and I want . . .* Using all three creates its effectiveness. "I feel uncomfortable when you call me 'sweetheart' and I'd prefer to be called Judy." Or, "I'm annoyed when we agreed to meet at twelve and you arrive at twelve thirty." Or, "I feel excited when our new team works together so effectively."

The first segment is using an "I" coupled with a feeling. The use of a feeling word adds to the depth and directness of the communication. When people are telling you how they feel, in response to you and your actions, it can be quite powerful. You can actually say "I feel," followed by the feeling word, or "I am," followed by the feeling word. Or you can even squeak by with "It's annoying when . . ." although that's a bit less direct. The feeling can be positive or negative.

You follow the feeling word with a description of what

the behavior, situation, or action is that you are pleased or displeased about. The important distinction here is between a description of the action and a label about the action. So, for example, "when you are so rude" is a label, while "when you come fifteen minutes late to our team meetings and leave thirty minutes early" is a description. Putting the first two segments together might sound like, "I get ticked off when you come fifteen minutes late to our team meetings and leave thirty minutes early."

The third segment is the critical one: telling what you want. You can begin this segment with any kind of statement of preference: "I'd like," "I'd prefer," "I'd choose," "I want." You then follow with a clear and specific desired outcome. "I'd like you to report back to me Tuesday at eight." "I'd prefer that we meet at my office, rather than yours." "I'd rather that you bring the overhead projector to the presentation." Again, brevity and the three-segment approach to telling what you want is a very easy and broadly applicable direct communication approach.

Although there may certainly be other techniques that could qualify as direct and/or assertive, the ones mentioned here are an adequate foundation for readers who need to build a sound direct influence infrastructure before they move on to the more advanced indirect communication approach.

Cut to the Chase

■ Direct communication is the traditional style of U.S. business, but not that of many other countries and cultures.

■ Directness was popularized and extended to personal conversation as "assertive communication" beginning in the late 1960s.

■ American business leaders need to be steeped in skills

of directness before they can use indirect influence techniques effectively.

■ There are innumerable ways to communicate directly. This chapter describes six: saying no, making "I" statements, being brief and specific, making statements rather than asking questions, broken record, and telling what you want.

Notes

1. F. Fournies, *Why Employees Don't Do What They're Supposed to Do: And What to Do About It* (New York: Liberty Hall Press, 1988).
2. J. Steil and J. Hillman, "The Perceived Value of Direct and Indirect Influence Strategies: A Cross-Cultural Comparison," *Psychology of Women Quarterly* 17:2 (1993), pp. 457–62.
3. R. Alberti and M. Emmons, *Your Perfect Right: A Guide to Assertive Living*, 7th ed. (San Luis Obispo, CA: Impact Publishers, 1995).
4. From N. Josefowitz, *Paths to Power* (Reading, MA: Addison-Wesley, 1980).
5. See F. Trompenaars, *Riding the Waves of Culture* (London: The Economist Books Ltd., 1993).

Chapter 4

Indirect Influence

Sophisticated and Subtle

Following a speech I delivered recently on indirect influence techniques, a participant came up to me and said, "I don't know what you're talking about. Maybe because I've always considered myself the Queen of Directness, but still . . . why in the world would anyone want to be indirect when they could be direct? What a waste of time to even bother! I don't get it." She voiced what many assertive and aggressive people may think. Their perception is based on the belief that to-the-point, cut-to-the-chase, say-it-like-it-is communication is always the best and the most fitting technique for all influence situations and, if you don't use it in most situations, something must be wrong with you, or with your thinking.

In my first days as a therapist, I learned that the direct influence approach often doesn't work and that insight doesn't produce change. My brilliant interpretations might have been inspiring, but didn't bring about new behaviors. And I found that nobody ever did what I said when I gave them specific detailed answers to their questions. "Should I stay with her or leave her?" "Should I keep my job or look for another?" "Should I choose this potential partner or that one?"

I learned that even when people were paying me to tell them what to do, there was a strong and basic resistance to being given advice, suggestions, and opinions. Consciously or not, many people feel better when they believe that what they're choosing to do is their own idea, not yours. They respond better when they don't recognize that someone is purposefully attempting to influence them. Perhaps the resistance to directness is as much a part of our heritage as rebels, pioneers, and entrepreneurs as is the direct style itself. Or perhaps it's just a consequence of the changing times, changing demographics, and changing workforce in the United States.

Although directness seems to be more frequently seen as ineffective and unwise in the U.S. business culture, it is still accepted and acceptable. Directness is not an accepted value in many other cultures, however. In these other varied cultures, receptive or indirect influence is more prevalent than expressive or direct influence. Listening is seen as smart and being subtle is valued more than being explicit, according to K. C. Chan-Herur. "Don't you think this is a good idea?" is generally viewed as preferable to "I need you to do this."[1]

A participant in one of my workshops, Norwald, told a story of working for several years in Saudi Arabia, a country that values indirect influence. He learned through experience that when he wanted something in particular—for example, to check on documentation for an expected expatriate employee of the corporation—he needed to go to the correct office and hang around for an hour or two. While chatting and drinking tea, Norwald would make pleasant conversation with the people there and have discussions about weather or vacations, business or news, but he would never ask for anything. After a randomly irregular period of time, one man in particular would say to him, "Before you leave, is there anything I can do for you?" Norwald would act surprised, and as if he had just remembered that he did need something, would reply, "Oh, yes. Thank you for asking. As long as I'm here I thought I might find out how the paperwork is moving along on our new employee, Sanford Stoyle." The response would be gracious and helpful. "Actually, I was just checking on that this morning and everything is in order. It is proceeding smoothly."

In the more indirect cultures, individuals tend to place more responsibility on the receiver than the sender to determine the full intent of the message. The receiver has to put together the puzzle and figure out how to respond. The sender doesn't have to design or define the message clearly. This is certainly an added reason why we all need to get better at reading people, and at reading them within their context, which may be their culture, their personality, or their relationship environment with their manager and team.

Intelligent leaders will begin to recognize that indirect influence skills are more sophisticated, versatile, and often more effective in bringing about a desired outcome, while at the same time avoiding barriers, than the direct influence approach. Broadening your communication repertoire to increase your influence span is the goal of learning about indirect influence and the "Beyond Assertiveness" approach.

What "Beyond Assertiveness" Is

"Beyond Assertiveness" (BA) refers to the planned use of specific verbal indirect influence techniques to accomplish desired outcomes—specifically, to get people to do what you want them to do. The communication techniques are devised purposefully and intentionally on the part of the influencer, but not seen as intentional influencing techniques by the target person.

The BA approach can be open or closed, meaning clearly seen and heard, if not understood, as in the Paradox or Matching techniques, or somewhat hidden and embedded, as in Modeling or Reframing (these techniques will be covered later in this chapter). However, in general, this approach is considered closed because the influencer is masking the fact that he or she is purposefully attempting to influence a target person. The intention to influence in a specific way is always hidden, even if the technique used is seen and heard openly. For example, if you're telling a story, your audience will see you and hear you openly. However, they probably won't know that you have identified a specific outcome that you want to achieve with that story.

If you tell your audience your intention and your point, you are no longer using the "Beyond Assertiveness" approach. You are attempting to influence the group directly and openly. BA is less than open, without being dishonest, for a specific reason. You don't want the target person to know what you want as a goal, lest you generate resistance, defensiveness, and opposition. BA is a win-win situation because, even when the speaker gets what she wants, the target person doesn't lose.

People have undoubtedly been using indirect influence techniques for years, under different names. A quote from *Wild Swans*, a book about life in China in the early 1900s, illustrates the use of an indirect influence approach: "My great-grandfather knew that his approach to General Xue had to be indirect. An explicit offer of his daughter's hand would lower her price, and there was also the possibility that he might be turned down. . . . In those days, respectable women could not be introduced to strange men, so Yang had to create an opportunity for General Xue to see his daughter. The encounter had to seem accidental."[2] This was an intentional influence attempt, but indirect. The influencer saw that the desired outcome could be achieved only if the meeting were viewed as unintentional by General Xue.

BA and Therapy

The literature of therapy holds information about the purpose and value of indirect communication as an influence technique. An article by Jerome Gans, "The Leader's Use of Indirect Communication in Group Therapy," identifies indirect communication as a leadership technique designed for those situations in which the leader must respond immediately, but where doing so directly might be a clinical mistake. The reasons Gans gives for preferring indirectness in many situations are very similar to the reasons discussed in Chapter 2: existing resistance among group members, concern about creating defensiveness or hostility, timing, the individual's expected acceptance, and the leader's comfort with different types of influence.[3]

Therapy, as currently viewed, and even as historically conceived, is definitely a social influence process, relying on many of the same principles as other social influence situations such as selling, managing, and ordinary interpersonal communication. It makes sense then that many indirect influence techniques originated, or at least were labeled as such, through therapy. As the various specific techniques of "Beyond Assertiveness" are discussed in the following chapters, the contribution of a particular therapeutic mode to the development of that technique is also discussed.

The first theorist and therapist to have a major impact, pioneering the use of a broad spectrum of indirect influence techniques aimed at behavior change, was Milton Erickson. A psychiatrist living in Phoenix, he was a doctor who was viewed as "far out" by his medical colleagues, and ultimately was more embraced by psychologists than by physicians. His ideas and uses of indirect influence are cited in several chapters of this book. Erickson's work is described well in Jay Haley's *The Psychiatric Techniques of Milton Erickson, M.D.: Uncommon Therapy* and Sidney Rosen's *My Voice Will Go with You: The Teaching Tales of Milton H. Erickson.*

BA and Business

Management and leadership both rely heavily on the social influence process to achieve desired outcomes, even though their roles may differ. The best leaders have a high need for power and a high concern for influencing people. The need for power, however, is not directed toward controlling others, or motivated by ego, or a concern for personal power. McClelland and Burnham, authors of an article called "Power Is the Great Motivator," suggest that acting like a coach rather than like an authority figure works best to influence people: "Don't force people to do things, help them to figure out ways of getting things done."[4] Sounds like they're advocating indirect influence to me.

Very little has been written or researched about the value, not to mention the power, of indirect influence, either perceived or actual, in the business environment. Recently, however, support for the BA approach has begun to emerge in articles about communication and diversity. This makes perfect sense as we recognize the increasingly diverse workforce in the United States and the fact that many other cultures don't embrace direct influence.

An article in the *Managing Diversity Newsletter*, "Giving Feedback in a Diverse Environment," doesn't use the same language used in this book, but the authors, Gardenswartz and Rowe, talk about indirect influence. They note that one of the biggest obstacles to giving employees feedback, and achieving the desired results, is too much directness. Their suggestions for giving feedback in a diverse environment (and all environments are diverse these days) all rely on more indirect communication, particularly for employees from business cultures other than that of the United States. The authors mention that direct feedback may be perceived as a shameful event that causes loss of face. An indirect response avoids that discomfort and embarrassment, as well as the possible resulting shutdown of the manager-employee relationship.

Gardenswartz and Rowe also point out that people from group-oriented cultures may find discomfort in having their performance singled out, in any way, negatively or positively. A more indirect and more private approach may work to fit these employees' needs. They also propose making statements that are more implicit than explicit and using passive rather than active voice as good ways to be more indirect. For example, "The project isn't complete and the deadline is today" may work better than "You didn't complete the project on time."[5]

In part, the apparent lack of awareness of the utility of "Beyond Assertiveness" in business may be due to difficulty observing or identifying an indirect influence technique. You usually don't know what's going on in the head of the influencer, unless it's you. I asked many managers about indirect influence and few seemed to know or want to guess, right off the bat. There was almost some embarrassment or dubiousness about whether it really was okay to be an indirect influencer as a manager. But when I explained BA briefly to managers, as well as positioned indirect influence as something positive, used by smart people, many of them were able to give good and real examples of how they had already used it.

Jim Dodenhoff, a senior manager, gave a good definition. He said indirect influence is giving nondirect cues or motivators to create desired actions or outcomes. He sees the use of

"Beyond Assertiveness" as somewhat of a political process involving massaging and balancing of egos. He says it's best used when, as a manager:

- You're so angry that you're going to rip somebody apart.
- You're so associated with a cause that your directness can be offensive to the other side.
- The person or group you're trying to influence thinks in nonlinear fashion.
- The other person or group doesn't trust you, or doesn't trust anybody.[6]

All these points can be subsumed under the general category of situations where, as a manager, you believe your audience is or will be resistant, oppositional, or defensive.

A Comparison: Before and beyond Assertiveness

In some situations, the observable behavior of the indirect influencer, using the "Beyond Assertiveness" approach, may appear exactly the same as the observable behavior of the non-assertive person. What makes the behavior entirely different, however, is that the nonassertive person does, says, or doesn't do or say what he wants, because he fears the consequences of a direct approach. The Beyond Assertive influencer behaves as he does because he has chosen the approach as the best way to handle a given situation, influence a specific person, and get that person to do what the influencer wants done.

Here's an example. Marra, a before-assertiveness (or nonassertive) person, asked her boss for some feedback about a proposal she had submitted several weeks earlier. He had answered, "Sure," and she hadn't heard another word in two weeks. Although she was concerned and frustrated about not hearing anything, she feared pushing him and instead stewed about his anticipated disapproval, feeling sure that he had not liked it or he would have given her feedback sooner. She said nothing.

Selia, a Beyond Assertiveness person, in the same situation, said nothing from the beginning about feedback, assuming instead that her boss was satisfied with the results—if he weren't, he would have gotten back to her sooner. Behaviorally, both women acted the same, but they didn't feel the same. In this situation, although the boss probably wasn't influenced one way or the other by his employee's silence, Selia came across as more confident than Marra, if nonverbally and indirectly, increasing the likelihood that the boss would not get picky about the proposal.

Let's take the same example one step further. Marra continues to say nothing while she stews, but Selia decides she wants to use an indirect influence technique rather than a direct technique to get an answer. The direct approach would have been, "I'm concerned that I haven't received feedback about the proposal and I'd like to set a date to talk about it." But instead, she chooses indirectness because she recognizes that giving feedback on her proposal is low on her boss's priority list and that asking or telling him what she wants will be perceived as a sign of her insecurity and thus reduce her credibility. She chooses to reframe his lack of feedback as acceptance rather than rejection, low priority, or indifference, and says, "I've concluded that you're satisfied with the proposal for Program One of the diversity series of satellite broadcasts. I'm in the middle of Program Two now and will be turning that in on the fifth."

Clearly, she is attempting to influence him toward telling her whether he has any comments or concerns so she can incorporate those changes into Program Two. But her method is indirect—she's not asking, she's not telling, she's not convincing, reasoning, or stating the importance of what she wants. She does want something, though. She wants to know that her boss accepts her proposal for Program One so she can proceed with Program Two and not have to revamp it after the fact. In this indirect way, she gets an answer. She's not losing or being one-down. He's not losing or being manipulated. She gets what she wants and yet avoids some of the negative feelings or perceptions she might get as feedback if she used a direct approach.

What "Beyond Assertiveness" Isn't

It's Not Nonassertive Communication

Here's an example of a conversation that demonstrates indirect, but nonassertive, communication on the part of a manager, Lars, talking to a team member, Stew. This is not Beyond Assertiveness. It demonstrates the use of avoidance, vagueness, and evasion. As you read this conversation, see if you can figure out what Lars wants to say or what outcome he wants to accomplish.

Lars: How do you think your team meeting went yesterday?

Stew: It went okay except for a couple of rough spots.

Lars: These meetings are very important. And they need to go well. Does the team understand what they need to do? Or do we need to give them more answers?

Stew: I think we're all right. Some guys can really nitpick. But a few said they appreciated the meeting.

Lars: Maybe, but I think we might want to give them more information.

Stew: Let's wait and see what comes down.

Lars: I'm not sure that's the best way to deal with it.

Lars seems to express concern about the effectiveness of the team meeting, but he doesn't say so. Stew seems to experience some defensiveness about the effectiveness of the team meeting, but he doesn't say so either. Do you think either of these men was influenced by the other? Probably not. My guess is that absolutely nothing happened as a result of the conversation. Lars's communication can't even be considered an influence attempt, because he apparently hadn't planned for a desired outcome, nor had he intentionally chosen an indirect influence technique. This was not an indirect influence attempt. This was plain old nonassertiveness.

Hinting is another way to go as a nonassertive communicator. "It would be great if I had more new clients who would be as satisfied as you are." This is indirect communication, but it is not indirect influence because the receiver probably doesn't do what you want. He or she doesn't know what you want. And it is not the "Beyond Assertiveness" approach. You as the speaker lose, or at least don't win, and you don't act on what you want—a sin of omission, or nonassertiveness.

It's Not Manipulation

Another common thought about indirect communication is that if you're not a wimp, and you still use indirectness, then you must be manipulative—implying deviousness in meeting your own needs at the expense of someone else's. Here's a conversation that demonstrates indirect, but manipulative, communication on the part of a manager, Kurt, dealing with the same problem and person Lars dealt with:

Kurt: So Stew, how do you think your team meeting went?

Stew: It went okay, except for a couple of rough spots.

Kurt: Mmm. Do you think the team felt good about how you ran it and what was accomplished?

Stew: I think we're all right.

Kurt: Did you get any direct feedback?

Stew: Well, you know some guys always nitpick.

Kurt: Yeah, I do know that. In fact, I heard those guys saying what a lousy job you do running those meetings and what a waste of time they are for everyone involved. I'm tired of this lack of awareness you seem to have, Stew. It's time to get real here, buddy. Time to shape up.

In this situation, Kurt is apparently trying to influence Stew to "confess" about his poor performance. He's asking questions, in an indirect way, rather than telling Stew directly what his concern is and what he wants. Ultimately, he expresses his anger, puts Stew down, and takes the opportunity to "punish" Stew in a definite win-lose scenario. He uses interrogation and accusation to beat Stew. Kurt's communication can't be considered a "Beyond Assertiveness" approach, because it is not a win-win. This is not an indirect influence attempt. It's plain old aggressiveness and manipulation.

Manipulation is an approach to influence that is by definition closed, indirect, dishonest, and win-lose. Manipulators conceal their objective. They may use direct or indirect communication but don't tell you what they really want.

A business acquaintance asked to attend one of my Genderflex workshops and conduct some before-and-after research on the value of the program for participants. I agreed. She did just that with my cooperation and help. Subsequently, she began to conduct her own workshops on gender communication in the workplace, although to my knowledge she had no related experience other than what she learned through my presentations.

Initially, she had told me that what she wanted was to conduct research. Ultimately, however, it appeared that what she wanted was to use my material to compete with me. She won. I felt conned. Manipulation may work successfully once or twice, but ultimately the target person catches on and doesn't trust again—at least not that person or his motives.

It's Not Influencing through Other People in Power

Indirect influence is also not, at least not in the context of this book, the effective use, or ineffective use for that matter, of other people's power to get what you want. The tactics of "one hand washes the other," or asking powerful people to intervene on your behalf, or to support your initiative, are all too often associated with politics as ways to increase potential influence. You may have similar interests and motivation, or shared trust with the high-powered person. You may have the expertise, but they may have the position of power that it takes to get something done. When you help them to achieve their position, they are more likely to use their influence to help you achieve your goal.

This use of other people is indirect in the sense that your influence attempt goes through someone else rather than directly from you to the target person or group. It can sometimes be seen as manipulative, but often it is just a good way to get things done, and no one ends up the loser. But it's not an indirect influence technique.

It's Not "The Flounce"

An article in *Savvy* magazine titled "How Southern Belles Outsmart City Slickers" addresses the soft, beat-around-the-bush approach used so successfully by southern women. The author of the article disdains eye-batting as overdone and offensive, but suggests that you don't have to fight fire with fire, nor always ride into town shooting. Moseying around the point is just good negotiating, from her viewpoint.[7]

"The Flounce" is a technique that works when moseying around hasn't made a dent. It's a blend of aggression and femininity and might sound something like this: "I can't believe you're backing out on the deal. I'm hurt, I'm crushed, I swear this is upsetting me to death. I trusted you like a brother. How could you possibly let me down like this? I was counting on you to be a gentleman, to be honorable, and you've just turned into a downright scoundrel before my very eyes." Imagine this with a southern accent and the addition of fitting nonverbal behavior, and you can feel the potential power!

It's definitely extreme, certainly southern, and from my point of view, definitely manipulative, which is why it and its sister techniques don't qualify as indirect influence techniques under the BA umbrella.

The Differences: Before Assertiveness, Assertiveness, Manipulation, and beyond Assertiveness

Let's look at the basic differences between nonassertiveness (or before assertiveness), assertiveness (or direct influence), manipulation, and Beyond Assertiveness (or indirect influence). Nonassertiveness is closed, indirect, generally dishonest, and lose-win—the speaker loses the conversation or nonconversation because she isn't even attempting to ask for, tell, or get what she wants. With assertiveness, you are open, direct, honest, and win-win. You use direct influence techniques to accomplish your communication goals, as discussed in the last chapter.

If you want your clients to refer more business to you, say so directly: "I'm delighted that you're so happy with your investments. I would like you to consider giving me the names of three friends or acquaintances of yours who might also like to increase their comfort with investing." If you only hint around, they'll probably never refer anyone to you—if only because they don't know what you want.

Let's take a common workplace situation and determine how it would be handled by someone using each of the four approaches. George is a stockbroker. The market is volatile, and one of George's long-term clients, a woman approaching retirement, is getting nervous about one IRA that is invested predominantly in stocks. She calls George and tells him that she's thinking about liquidating her assets and reinvesting them in bonds. George doesn't think this is a good idea. He thinks his client should stay in the same IRA and ride out the volatility.

If George is a nonassertive communicator, he might agree, unenthusiastically, to do what the client wants and never mention his opinion: "Okay, Judy, if that's what you want." Or he might make a hinting, indirect comment: "The market probably will stabilize in the next few months."

If he concludes that the direct approach would work best with Judy, and he is assertive, George might say, "I understand your concern about the safety of your retirement money and I have some thoughts about what's the best thing to do. I think, in the long run, it would be best to stay with the stocks. I'd like to discuss the decision with you in detail. What would work best for you? My office or yours?" He's direct, open, honest, and win-win in this discussion. He's not trying to overrun Judy, but he's trying to influence her to stay with the current asset allocation and delay her decision until he has a chance to influence her further to keep her stocks.

If George is a manipulator, he might instead say, "That's a very conservative decision to make. I thought you were more of a risk-taker than that, but I guess as you're getting older, you're getting more afraid of losing the money." This approach isn't helpful to Judy, and depending on her particular history and response to George, she may be intimidated into leaving the IRA in stocks. George gets what he wants. Judy doesn't. Or she could feel insulted and decide to find another financial adviser. A possible losing result for both George and Judy.

If, instead, George decides that an indirect technique will work best, because he recognizes that Judy is somewhat of an oppositional person, he could say, "Thanks for bringing this up. I hadn't been thinking about your getting closer to retirement and wanting to be safer. We probably should get together to review your whole investment and retirement picture to be sure we're where you want to be and where it's most comfortable for you to be." George is going along with what Judy says she wants, yet not saying what he wants. It is, in a way, closed communication. It's indirect and not totally honest, although not dishonest, and it is a win-win situation, moving perhaps to another win-win when the meeting actually takes place.

Women and Men

Research cited in *Sex Differences and Similarities in Communication*, by Canary and Dindia, notes that both high- and low-credibility influencers can use indirectness, or what the authors call "low-intense appeals," successfully. They comment that in the United States the expectation is that men can be more effective with direct, or "high-intense," and even aggressive attempts at persuasion, while women can be more persuasive with low-intense and unaggressive messages. Generally, Americans view individuals using direct strategies as more powerful and self-confident than individuals employing indirect strategies. The questions arise: Are women seen as less powerful because they use indirect techniques? Or do they use indirect techniques because they know they're viewed as less powerful? And do men use direct techniques because they know they're seen as powerful? Or are they viewed as powerful because they use direct influence techniques?[8]

From my point of view, the research just described doesn't take into account the important factors of audience, relative power, and timing. Men can perhaps be more effective with men using direct communication, and women can be more effective with men using indirect communication. Some research by Linda Carli suggests that women aren't well accepted by women in the indirect mode, but are more effective with men being indirect.[9] I wonder if that finding is based on traditional models of gender roles, on comfort, or on some conflict between the old sex-role stereotypes and the new.

Newer research by Carli on influence, gender, and communication looked at the effect on a same- and opposite-gender audience of different styles of influence. In this study, a male and a female confederate delivered a persuasive message using a high-task, social, submissive, or dominant nonverbal style. The high-task style was characterized by firm tone of voice, high eye contact, upright posture, and rapid rate of speech. The social nonverbal style included a friendly, relaxed facial expression, moderate voice volume, average eye contact, and relaxed posture. The submissive style was characterized by a hesitant, soft, and pleading voice, nervous gestures, and little eye contact. In contrast, the dominant style was portrayed with a loud and angry voice, stern facial expression, pointing gestures, and almost consistent eye contact.

The social and high-task styles were more influential, across gender, than the dominant. But men only liked women who were high-task if they were also social, meaning they smiled, looked friendly and relaxed, had high eye contact, were occasionally hesitant, and used a moderate tone of voice. Carli interpreted this finding to mean that women need to communicate that there is no desire to usurp male power with their task style. They can do this by combining it with a social style. Men can be influential to men and women, in the high-task style, without adding components of the social style.[10]

My own hypothesis, based on the theory that people are more readily influenced by people they see as similar to themselves, is that women will be more effective with men if they are more direct than they might normally be, and men will be more effective with women if they are less direct. Informal research I conducted with hundreds of business men and women workshop participants identified "listening" as the communication behavior most women would like more of from men—certainly an indirect influence approach—and "getting to the point" as the behavior most men would like more of from women—certainly a direct approach.

How to Use Indirectness

The first step for many people in preparing to use indirect communication, as it is with people attempting to use direct communication, is to get rid of the negative thinking that invades their brains and sometimes prevents them from acting: "This won't work." "He won't get it." "She'll just keep on doing what she's doing." "This is wimpy." "Is this being manipulative?" "Is this a cop-out?" "Am I just trying to avoid confrontation?" "He'll think I'm weird, not just getting directly to the point." Eliminating this kind of thinking is essential to success in making any kind of purposeful influence attempt. Once you're thinking neutrally rather than negatively, your fear of consequences decreases and you're confident enough to use the techniques.

Once you've rid yourself of the negative thinking, you can go back to The Drill, go through the steps, and perhaps arrive more frequently at indirectness as the best choice to use with a person in a specific situation. Then you can move on to review the array of techniques available to you and, after reading the following chapters in the book, determine which one or ones will work best for which people and situations.

Beyond Assertiveness: The Indirect Influence Techniques

The indirect influence techniques that this book addresses specifically are: Modeling and Matching, Acting in Accord, Reframing, Paradox, Confusing, the Columbo Approach, Storytelling and Metaphor, and Humor.

Modeling and Matching

Modeling is behaving in the ways you want others to match. Your behavior becomes the model for others to imitate. *Matching* refers to a planned generation of verbal and nonverbal behavior which matches that of another person. As they sense or feel the similarities between the two of you, they are more readily influenced by you. This is a very simple concept that is not quite so easy to translate into action without over- or underdoing the match. If your target person leans back, looks up at the ceiling and says "Hmmm," your matching behavior might be to lean back slightly and look up at the ceiling as well, but omit the verbal behavior.

Acting in Accord

When you *act in accord*, you give the person you want to influence what he wants and needs from you, as long as you're not selling your soul to do so. When the target person says to you, "You are being condescending to me," you can act in accord by responding: "Perhaps I did sound a bit patronizing," recognizing that what they want is acknowledgment. Many times we, as managers and potential influencers, want what we want on general competitive or authoritative principles, but not for a good business reason. We become oppositional to the person we are trying to influence, not "giving in" to her wishes even if her actual want is easy for us to grant.

Acting in Accord is simply giving her what she appears to want or need.

Reframing

Reframing is the process of communicating in such a manner that you alter the way in which the target person perceives events, in order to change the meaning. When the meaning changes, the person's responses and behaviors also change. For example, if you are counseling someone about a complaint related to sexual harassment and he becomes vehement in denying that he has harassed anyone, you might downgrade your wording to something like "You may have been unintentionally discriminating against Sophia." Although that phrase, strictly speaking, is not the same as possible sexual harassment, you may help reduce the person's resistance enough so he can hear you by reframing his behavior in this way.

Paradox

According to the dictionary, *paradox* has multiple meanings, but for the purposes of this book it is most closely defined as a statement that seems contradictory, unbelievable, or absurd, but which may actually be true. A paradoxical communication is totally contrary to expectations. In the therapy context, a paradoxical statement is often used as a way of putting someone in a double bind in order to initiate change. The paradox may be a directive that the therapist gives in which he actually wants the person to resist, in order to create change. For example, telling someone who is worried about the fact that he worries all day to work harder at worrying and spend an hour a day on focused worrying instead of eight hours on unfocused worrying is a paradoxical directive. This indirect influence technique may be the most difficult for a manager to understand and implement in the workplace context, but is extremely powerful and fun to use.

Confusing

Confusing is an indirect influence technique that originally comes from the therapeutic communication lingo of hypnosis. You, as the speaker, can choose to use confusion to influence the listener to come up with her own answer or solution to a problem, her own vision or plan, her own idea or creative thought about her situation. When you speak to them in a somewhat confusing, rambling manner, people's tendency is to turn you off, stop listening, go inside their minds and think things through in their own way while you're still rattling on. This is particularly useful when you want people to take more initiative, to be more independent, but don't want to tell them to be that way directly because that is like telling people to be spontaneous. By the very act of telling them to be that way, you take away their opportunity to do so.

The Columbo Approach

This indirect influence technique could also be called the "confused" approach, but to avoid the confusion of differentiating the Confusing technique from the confused approach, I call it the *Columbo approach*. It is the art of acting confused yourself—rather than causing confusion—also known as "playing dumb." Donald Meichenbaum, a well-known Canadian psychologist, coined the term to describe an indirect influence approach he uses instead of interrogating clients to get the facts. The name comes from the 1970s TV program in which Peter Falk played an apparently inept detective, Lieutenant Columbo. By asking many questions, emanating from a one-down rather than one-up position, he demonstrated an amazing ability to garner vital information that he'd never have gathered with a more direct or competitive approach.

Storytelling and Metaphor

Storytelling is a way to influence people indirectly by telling them a story—without necessarily telling them the point of the story, before or after, and letting them come to their own conclusions. Many classic fairy tales, such as "The Emperor's New Clothes," have embedded powerful messages that are never stated. I told stories without making my point overtly in Chapter 1 of this book. Whether you're telling a story or not, leaving the point of your communication unstated, keeping it unfinished business, is often a good way to influence people. They don't resist you because you give them nothing to resist. They come up with their own directive, taken from what you have said.

A *metaphor* is a statement about one thing that resembles something else. It is a statement that contains an implied comparison—for example, your boss tells you you're the quarterback for development of a new product line. Many stories contain metaphors or are metaphors, but you can also have a metaphor outside of a story.

Humor

Humor is perceiving, appreciating, or expressing what is funny or amusing in a situation. Humor influences people to feel differently and to see events from a different perspective. Humor puts people at ease, equalizes situations and relationships, increases creativity and group rapport. Humor alone can accomplish many indirect influence goals.

Take a Pass at Indirect

■ Often, people resist being told what to do, how to do it, or receiving unsolicited advice.

■ When you use indirect influence, your intention is to

influence target people, without their recognizing your intention. That's how and why it works.

■ Indirect influence is not manipulation and it's not non-assertiveness.

■ There are uncountable different ways to indirectly influence others. This book illustrates eight techniques: Matching, Acting in Accord, Reframing, Paradox, Confusing, The Columbo Approach, Storytelling and Metaphor, and Humor.

Notes

1. See K. C. Chan-Herur and C. Evans, "Dealing Effectively with Cross-Cultural Issues in Influence and Negotiation" (Berkeley, Ca.: Barnes and Conti Associates, Inc., 1994).
2. From Jung Chan, *Wild Swans: Three Daughters of China* (New York: Doubleday, 1991).
3. See J. Gans, "The Leader's Use of Indirect Communication in Group Therapy," *International Journal of Group Therapy* 46:2 (1996), pp. 209–228.
4. See D. McClelland and D. Burnham, "Power Is the Great Motivator," *Harvard Business Review*, January–February 1995, pp. 126–139.
5. See L. Gardenswartz and A. Rowe, "Giving Feedback in a Diverse Environment," *Managing Diversity Newsletter* 6:12 (September 1997), pp. 1, 4.
6. J. T. Dodenhoff, "Interpersonal Attraction and Direct-Indirect Supervisor Influence as Predictors of Counselor Trainee Effectiveness," doctoral dissertation, Arizona State University, May 1978.
7. See K. W. Wiley, "How Southern Belles Outsmart City Slickers," *Savvy*, July 1985, pp. 48–52.
8. See D. Canary and K. Dindia, *Sex Differences and Similarities in Communication* (Mahwah, NJ: Laurence Erlbaum Associates Publishers, 1998).
9. L. Cami, "Gender, Language, and Influence," *Journal of Personality and Social Psychology*, 59:11 (1990), pp. 941–951.
10. See L. Carli, S. La Fleur, and C. Loeber, "Nonverbal Behavior, Gender, and Influence," *Journal of Personality and Social Psychology* 68:6 (1995), pp. 1030–1041.

Chapter 5

Modeling and Matching

The Similarity Bias Par Excellence

Modeling and Matching are two sides of the same indirect influence technique. When you model the behavior you want others to follow, you are influencing them to do what you want them to do—by indirectly showing them how to be like you. When you match others' behavior, you are indirectly influencing them to do what you want them to do—by being like them.

Modeling and Matching are techniques that can be used in leadership, in sales and management, in parenting, and in personal relationships. The concept is simple, based on a sound social psychological principle. We are all more readily influenced by people we see as similar to ourselves. Whether this "similarity bias" happens automatically, unconsciously, or with our full awareness, social psychological research supports the principle that we are more easily influenced by people we like, feel comfortable with, and perceive as similar to ourselves. Think of how many conversations with strangers begin with an unspoken search to find something in common. If we find commonality right away, we usually stay on the topic for a long time, before moving to another. For example, people who don't know each other often inquire about where the other person is from as a way to get things started. Just yesterday, a workshop participant asked that question and when I responded "Arizona," he said "Oh, my nephew lives in Arizona." And off we went discussing Arizona, even though the man had never been there, didn't want to go there, and knew little about it, not even where in Arizona his nephew lived. But it was something, however slight, that we had in common so we stuck to it for a good five minutes. Perhaps we fear that this similarity may be the only one we'll find—and we'll be reduced to silence if we don't come upon another. Or it may mean that we need to talk about some of our differences.

If we don't find similarities in interests, geography, family, or sports teams right off the bat, we may wander endlessly from pets to children, from ethnicity to occupation, from favorite movie to best vacation spot, in order to hopefully arrive at commonality. Once there, no matter how far the stretch, we can relax and enjoy the good feelings that come from being in sync and continue to build a relationship based on shared experience. Whew! We no longer have to worry about the unexpected, the unpredictable, and the unknown. This person is just like us!

If we don't establish similarity on any level, about any topic, then we are much less likely to be open to the influence of the other person and he is less likely to be influenced by us. It doesn't mean there's no hope, it just means it may take longer and require more finesse to make the similarity bias work for us.

Modeling

A friend, Dan Pickens, talks about his grandmother as a wonderful model for him. "She greeted people as if everyone came to her with a past. She understood and accepted people at a deep level. She molded my character. She molded my life without ever appearing to try to or without seeming to want to change me in any way. She always saw the good and was good. She never went negative with herself or with me, so I had to live up to her expectations. I had to raise my own expectations of myself—the expectations she had of herself and of me—that she communicated through her behavior."

Modeling is a powerful influence technique. To model is to serve as a pattern or standard of excellence to be imitated. In its simplest form, Modeling is the basis of much of what we learn as kids about being adults. In many ways, it is how we learn to behave in ways that are expected of our gender, our roles, and our culture. We see dads shave and moms put on lipstick, and we follow suit at play as boys and girls of three or four. We meet teachers or neighbors or other children whom we like or admire and we unconsciously imitate their way of talking or walking in order to be more like them. As kids and as adults, we may follow "good" or "bad" models, depending on who is present in our lives, whom we like and admire, and whom we view as leaders. In these situations, the model is often not purposefully behaving in ways that she wishes to be imitated. The model serves as a pattern, perhaps glad to be influential, perhaps unknowing of her influence, but generally without the planned intention to be an influence.

You can also use third-person Modeling as an indirect influence technique. It's done all the time in advertising, and it can be used in day-to-day communication. When he was playing pro basketball, Magic Johnson was used to sell basketball shoes—he wore a certain brand and he was good, so the implication was that if you wore them you'd be good too. As Wyatt Earp, an insurance sales agent for New York Life, explained to me, Magic's name and fame can also be used today to encourage potential insurance clients to sign an agreement to have AIDS testing as a part of their qualifying for insurance. Magic signed. That's how he found out he was HIV positive. If he was brave enough to sign, then you should be too. There are many situations where you can talk about or show someone who's bigger than life, doing what you want your target person to do, and increase the impact through your use of third-party influence.

Modeling in its most complex form is well demonstrated by a brief example. At seventy-eight, Gandhi was asked, "What is your message?" He replied, "My life is my message." Gandhi presumably hoped to influence people through lifelong Modeling, but as a leader he probably didn't plan his daily activities primarily to inspire imitation. As a leader, he demonstrated such integrity between what he said and how he lived that his influence was global, then and now. He modeled a philosophy and a way of life that could be viewed as the ultimate use of indirect influence.

An Indian professor, Dr. Keshavan Nair, spoke at a recent conference about leadership and service. He quoted an Eastern saying: "When there's a great teacher, a student will appear." This idea can be extended to: When there's a great leader, followers will appear, and when there's a great model, imitators will appear. All three examples emphasize the essence and power of Modeling as an indirect influence technique.[1]

Unfortunately, as we all recognize, brutal leaders and other poor models can also produce a multitude of followers and imitators, with or without intent. When you model the "wrong" behavior, the behavior you don't want others to imitate, or "bad" behavior, meaning unethical behavior, there can be disastrous consequences.

We can all look around us today as well as historically and identify what we may deem unethical leadership behavior which was meticulously, zealously, and proudly followed: Hitler, Stalin, and Saddam Hussein are examples. In the context of the power of indirect influence, the purposeful Modeling of "ethical" behavior—desirable behavior that we want others to replicate—is obviously the focus.

However, recognizing the power of Modeling as indirect influence, whatever kind of behavior is being modeled, is extremely important. The CFO of a large manufacturing operation told a story about his CEO, Glenn, who didn't model active go-get-'em behavior and ended up with a management team that didn't work, literally and figuratively. He made pronouncements fairly frequently but he didn't act on them. He would say that sales were too slow and he was going to become the senior sales rep for the organization, get out there and press flesh, make it happen, bring in the business. But he kept on hanging around the office, talking, but not doing. People learned to watch what he did, not what he said he was going to do. He not only raised doubts and lost credibility by not Modeling the behavior he advocated, but he perpetuated a model of inactivity. The effect was catastrophic—the company died.

As a leader, if you model the desired behavior, you may be extremely effective in bringing about the desired behavior in others, even if you are not highly skilled as a communicator. When your colleagues like and admire you, they want to be like you, and they want to be liked by you. The similarity bias works to foster their imitation of your behavior. Wyatt Earp, the insurance agent mentioned earlier in this chapter, described a manager who influenced him strongly through Modeling.

The manager, Joe, used Storytelling and Modeling to bring about the outcome he desired—for agents to sell insurance, more frequently, to close friends and family, even though they were more reluctant to approach friends and family than strangers. Joe told a true story about the unexpected death of his close friend Lionel. Several months later, the widow said to Joe, "Why didn't you take responsibility for making sure Lionel was insured? You knew him well. You cared about him I know, but you didn't do your job for him—or for me. I don't understand how you could have let that happen." Joe felt tremendous remorse and guilt. But it helped him to get a different perspective on selling insurance to those people closest to him. In addition to talking about it, Joe also modeled it, in the office, on the golf course, at social gatherings, at sporting events. He was always selling, in a respectful, caring manner. He didn't push, but he always inquired about people's insurance knowledge and needs. In short order, everyone under Joe began to imitate that good behavior, willingly, enthusiastically, and effectively, without a direct influence attempt ever being made.

If you don't model the desired behavior as a leader, no matter how skilled you are in other direct or indirect communication techniques, you are less likely to influence people in the way you'd like. In a corporate setting, the surest way to decrease the possibility of sexual harassment becoming a problem is not for the human resources department or the CEO to loudly declare a zero tolerance policy, but rather for all the senior executives to demonstrate by their behavior that harassment in any way, shape, or form is unacceptable. That means no senior-level person publicly or privately tells a slightly off-color joke, leers at someone of the opposite sex, calls an employee "hon," "baby," or "doll," or flirts openly, subtly, or covertly with employees. It also means that written policies and procedures are distributed to all employees and training is provided regularly. The Modeling of the acceptable behavior is what has the most profound influence. It's walking the talk. It's showing that you mean what you say in a very unambiguous way.

Matching

Matching, the other side of the coin, refers to speakers' purposeful generation of verbal or nonverbal behavior that matches that of the people they're trying to influence. When you model, you want others to match your behavior, but when you match, you're purposefully behaving similarly to the target person. The goal is for the target person to sense or feel the similarity, without recognizing the intention, and therefore become more readily open to the speaker's influence. You can use Matching in a leading or following way—or both. Wyatt Earp says he starts off every meeting with a potential client, in a leading way, by demonstrating very open body language. His intent is for the client to match his body language, and consequently to feel open to Wyatt's message. Whether the client matches his openness or not, Wyatt moves into Matching the client's behavior, in a following way, after about five minutes.

Matching can be simple, but potent. Gary de Moss, a Van Kampen Mutual Funds marketing manager, was rare among my interviewees in his quick recognition of the use of indirect influence. He adroitly defined indirect influence as an intentional, but indirect, attempt to build or strengthen a relationship. The client or target person does not view the influence attempt as purposeful. He sees Matching, among other indirect influence techniques, as straightforward and smart rather than devious or manipulative in any way. Gary, who travels extensively, said that he uses Matching purposefully by dressing similarly to his clients. When he's in New York he wears cuff links and multicolored shirts. When he's in St. Louis he wears button-down blue or white oxford cloth shirts, all so that he appears similar to the client.

Matching can be as complicated a process as simultaneously using similar vocabulary, speaking at the same pace, and/or using intonation similar to the person you're trying to influence. You can add reflection of their nonverbal language. All these techniques are targeted to others who subconsciously may then view you as resonant with them.

Lisa Kueng, also in the marketing department of Van Kampen, uses Matching methods too. (Is it in the water or the mutual funds?) She says, somewhat ambivalently, that she seems to have an almost natural ability to take on some of the verbal and nonverbal communication modes of people with whom she associates in her business or personal life. As a teenager, she had a confrontation with a friend who became aware of Lisa's adaptive skill of Matching, and accused her of being phony. Lisa was crushed as a fifteen-year-old, but later was able to see her almost intuitive adaptability as a useful skill. She can talk sports analogies with the guys or use the music lingo when she describes a "kick-ass" restaurant to musician friends. She can change her vocabulary, her pace, and her stories to fit the group.

Specifically, what does that Matching behavior influence people to do? Maybe nothing more than to like Lisa, feel comfortable with her, and be open in the most general sense to her influence. Her Matching is like an influence deposit in the bank. She can make a withdrawal whenever she needs to because she has built up influence reserves.

Before ever talking to Lisa about indirect influence or knowing she used Matching quite purposefully, I was impressed with what an outstanding communicator she was. I was comfortable with her, I liked her, and I was open to her influence. Maybe she was already doing a good job of Matching with me, and I didn't realize it!

The Case

Duane was a new employee transferred by his company to the Phoenix office from Milwaukee. His manager, José, either wasn't comfortable with Duane or didn't know how to best manage him, although José thought, in general, that he was good at reading and adapting to people. Duane seemed to alternate between two extremes—very upbeat, positive, and even overenthusiastic behavior, followed by quiet, distant, and "blah" behavior. He overcommunicated when he was "up" and ceased communicating when he was "down." Sometimes his mode would seem to change on an hourly basis, sometimes on a daily basis. José found that sometimes a very direct influence approach worked well, while at other times the same approach seemed to generate resistance and even some stubbornness and controlled annoyance on Duane's part. Other people also seemed to have difficulty relating to Duane and found him unpredictable and changeable, although everybody generally seemed to like him, at least when he was positive and fun.

José felt a strong need to figure out how best to influence Duane for the benefit of the entire team. He felt like all eyes were upon him to determine how he was going to handle this apparently unmanageable employee while keeping the team running in the smooth way it had been functioning prior to Duane's arrival. Let's go back to "The Drill" to figure out how José could best work out this problem.

The Drill

■ *Decide what you want as an outcome of the communication.* In this situation, José wanted to gain a better understanding of Duane so that he could avoid the hit-and-miss successes of his past influence approaches. He wanted to figure out what was the best way to influence Duane overall, given that he was more unpredictable than most people José had worked with. José's ordinarily good people-reading skills weren't providing him with the information he wanted.

■ *Read the other person in the current situation.* Although he'd never used Matching as a way to gather information about someone else, or as an indirect influence technique, José decided this situation called for something unusual on his part. As is true for Beyond Assertiveness in general, as well as Matching in particular, reading the target person is the key to success. You can't match if you don't read the other person well. And while you're actually Matching, you inevitably learn more about the other person because you are acting like him. José had read previously about Neurolinguistic Programming (NLP) and the use of Matching in Bandler and Grinder's book *Frogs into Princes*, but went back to review the information so he could implement it successfully.[2] Here's what he found out.

NLP, a jazzy, but somewhat fringe approach to change through therapy, theorizes that people process information in different ways: visually, auditorily, or kinesthetically. Although people use all three senses to input information, NLP suggests that they tend to have a preferred mode which they demonstrate through the words they use and the eye movements they make. By Matching, or almost imitating, the other person's primary representational set, or way of processing information, you become temporarily more similar to her, and she senses, rather than become totally aware of, the commonality. Through the use of seeing, hearing, and feeling words, as well as nonverbal behavior, the influencer can establish a powerful persuasive connection.

People who are primarily "visual" prefer images, pictures, and color. They almost automatically translate words into images. If they can see ideas, if they can make an image in their minds, or if you can help them to get the picture, they'll be more ready to be influenced. You need to use language that will help them make quick pictures. Visual people see pictures in their minds and use words that reflect their visualization: They see what you mean, they get the picture, they focus, and ask you to illustrate points. They take a dim view, paint a picture, flash on, or get a bird's-eye view.

A second way of gauging others' representational sets is through their eye movements when they talk and think. According to the NLP experts, people who are visual tend to look up to either side as they're processing information. They may also just look straight ahead, as if they're envisioning a small screen between your eyes and theirs, and projecting images on it. Ask someone who you think is visual to spell a slightly difficult word, gregarious for example. Then watch their eye movements as they "see" the word in the air, on the ceiling, or on a visualized screen.

Auditory people hear what's going on. The sounds around them are what they use to help them process information. Kerry Johnson, in his audiotape *Sales Magic*, uses Jimmy Connors, the former tennis pro, as an example of an auditory person. Connors anticipates the strength and placement of his opponent's shots by hearing how the ball comes off the server's racket. Auditory people hear what you say: You ring a bell with them, a point is loud and clear, an idea lands with a thud. They give you an earful, ask you to give them your ear, they tune in and tune out and voice their opinions. Auditory people's eyes tend to stay at ear level, to either side as they think. If you ask them to spell a word, they are more likely to hear it in their head, rather than to see it.[3]

Kinesthetic people feel it all—they process information through their gut instead of their eyes or ears, the more commonly thought modes for inputting data. We may think of them as very emotional, but they actually just process data more on a feeling level than the average person. They rely on their intuition, their gut reaction, their sixth sense, to help them sort out information. Kinesthetic people get the drift: They feel your pain, they are floating, they send out trial balloons. They get a handle on things, hang in, start from scratch, and tell you to keep your shirt on.

Kinesthetic people look down, to either side, as they input and process data. They tend to process information viscerally or tactually. In recognition of this mode of processing information, preschools now have letters and numbers made out of fuzzy material or sandpaper, so that kids can feel what a *B* is or what a *6* feels like.

Everyone may, at one time or another, use all of these different kinds of words and phrases, and all of these types of eye movement, but if you listen and observe carefully, you'll notice that one mode predominates in an individual's use of visual, auditory, or kinesthetic language.

Although there is a dearth of research supporting NLP's theories, much of what NLP proponents say does fit with what we already know about social influence, similarity, and liking. The similarity bias says that we all tend to be more comfortable with, like more, and be more readily influenced by people we see as similar to ourselves. The obvious and most common ways of demonstrating similarity are by questioning people in a somewhat random way about their interests or background and hoping you can find something to pounce on. "No kidding, I played lacrosse in high school, too!" But the process can be tedious and appear contrived. Using eye movements and speaking words similar to those used by the target person, as NLP suggests, is much more subtle, and moves away from any suspicion of intentionality. People are often more open to influence when they don't think you are trying to influence them.

If you want to acquire some practice in guessing others' primary representational set, you need to fine-tune your observation and listening skills. Doing this is an excellent use of time because the more you know and understand about the target person, the better the chances are that you'll do a good job of influencing him or her. By listening and observing, you'll learn so much about the other person that you'll readily know, not only how to match them, but what influence approach and technique will work best.

Johnson suggests in *Sales Magic* that the best way to find out people's primary representational set is to ask them about their first hour of wakefulness. Ask them to focus on what they saw, heard, or felt. He speculates that people remember most about things they're most comfortable with, so they will remember most about what they saw if they're visual, what they heard if they're auditory, and what they felt if they're kinesthetic.[4]

You can also ask people some questions that are designed to elicit eye movements. Here's a sample series:

- Can and would you get a mental picture of an elephant's body with a giraffe's head and neck?
- Can and would you divide 262 by 12 in your head?
- Can and would you listen to "London Bridge Is Falling Down" in your head?
- Can and would you imagine yourself in the shower or the tub or a pool or the ocean feeling the water on your body?

As people answer, watch where their eyes move. Then, ask them at the end of the sequence which of the tasks was easiest for them. The question about the elephant is clearly visual, the one about "London Bridge" is loudly auditory, and the one about the shower feels kinesthetic. Often the easiest task indicates the person's primary representational set, and it is usually supported by the kind of eye movements he or she uses while processing the questions. If there's a mixed response, then you can use a mixed match.

Regardless of which method of gathering information you use for Matching, your customers or coworkers may notice and think you're weird, but they'll be intrigued. Tell them upfront that you're going to ask them a strange question or series of questions and that you'll explain later exactly what is the purpose. They'll be appreciative when you later explain that you're asking so you can do a better job of meeting their needs and communicating on their wavelength.

■ *Select an influencing method and technique—direct or indirect.* In the case of José and Duane, José's decision to use an indirect influence technique was made primarily because the direct approach hadn't worked well or consistently and he couldn't figure out his employee. Rather than stick with trial and error, José decided to do a reread and emphasize indirectness because there seemed to be a poor fit between the two men. Matching was the way he chose to reread Duane, with the idea that he would follow with a different indirect influence technique once he really understood Duane.

■ *Implement the technique.* José carried out his observation under the umbrella of getting to know Duane better in order to work more effectively together on the team. He determined that Duane was primarily kinesthetic, with a secondary high visual mode. Although he worked hard to match the language, the eye movements, and even some of the nonverbal behavior Duane exhibited, José found doing so to be extremely difficult because of Duane's vacillating moods and behavior. To match Duane was so unlike José's normal behavior that he found he really couldn't carry it off smoothly. As a matter of fact, matching Duane made José a wreck, but it did help him to understand something important about Duane. Matching was not going to work as an influence approach, but an indirect approach was definitely called for. José's other choice was resorting, if necessary, to a command-and-control approach which could work, some of the time, but would result in an oppositional employee, most of the time.

José decided the best thing to do was to model to Duane the behavior he wanted from him. Modeling was far less of a stretch than Matching Duane's behavior. Overall, José was very consistent, stable, low-key, but communicative, and always responsive in his relationship with Duane. He stayed in touch several times a day, by e-mail primarily, but also sometimes in writing and on the phone. Before he tried Matching, then intentional Modeling, he would sometimes get five or more long, rambling e-mails a day from Duane. On other days, he would e-mail Duane and get no response at all. Once José started Modeling the desired behavior, he would get prompt, brief responses to his e-mails, and an occasional lengthier but still more concrete and concise e-mail initiating a new topic or problem. After a while, seemingly in recognition of José's influence, Duane commented at a team meeting, "I've learned a lot from you, José. You've been good for me." José just smiled and commented that he was glad things were working out for Duane in Phoenix. End of conversation, and beginning of a successful indirect influence approach.

In sales and management, understanding the mental map of your internal or external customers always helps you to be more influential with them. According to Kerry Johnson, highly productive salespeople are able to sell the way their customers want to buy, whereas less successful salespeople sell as they want to be sold to.[5] The same principle applies to management. Managing the way that you want to manage, influencing the way that you want to be influenced, often doesn't work. Using what Tony Alessandra calls "The Platinum Rule" works best sometimes: Do unto others as they want done unto them, rather than using the Golden Rule and doing unto others as you want done unto you.[6]

Matching helps you as the influencer to get a good understanding of the target person's way of processing information. You have a leg up as an influencer with that information and the ability to match their way. Modeling, well done, shows others exactly what you want from them, so if they so choose, or are so moved to follow, they can adapt to you and do unto you as you'd like done unto you.

Copy Exactly

- Matching and Modeling are two of the most indirect and noninvasive BA techniques.

- Figuring out whether your customer is primarily visual, auditory, or kinesthetic is good people-reading practice, whether you use the information to match them or not.

- The similarity bias is extremely powerful. Use it well and subtly.

- Starting with indirect influencing styles and later moving to direct if indirect doesn't work is always better than vice-versa.

- As a leader, consistently Modeling the desired behavior is the most powerful way you can influence your employees.

Notes

1. K. Nair, "Leadership as Service," speech presented to the Valley of the Sun chapter of the American Society for Training and Development, Phoenix, Az., May 7, 1999.
2. R. Bandler and J. Grinder, *Frogs into Princes* (Moab, UT: Real People Press, 1979).
3. See K. Johnson, *Sales Magic* (audiotape) (Chicago: Nightingale Conant, 1990).
4. Ibid.
5. Ibid.
6. A. Alessandra and M. O'Connor, *The Platinum Rule* (New York: Warner books, 1996).

Chapter 6

Acting in Accord

Wise, Not Wimpy

Acting in Accord means to give the person what he wants and needs from you, as long as you're not selling your soul to do so. Its opposite is acting in discord, meaning to withhold from him, disagree with him, give him what he doesn't want from you, or fail to give him what he does do want from you.

Acting in Accord and Therapy

When I first began my practice as a therapist, I was a recent graduate of a Ph.D. program in counseling psychology, and a former psychiatric nurse. I was more experienced working with hospitalized mentally ill "patients" than somewhat neurotic, or even relatively healthy, "clients" who were proceeding stressfully through any one or more of life's tough transitions. I had never intended to be a therapist, but instead had studied to be a researcher and academician, so my focus had not been on the kinds of normal issues that often bring individuals and couples to a therapist. However, I quickly noticed a reoccurring theme.

Couples would arrive for counseling and they would all start out with the same opening request: "Dr. Tingley, we would like your honest and open opinion about whether our marriage can be saved. If not, we would really like to know now, rather than spending months of time and a lot of money pursuing a lost cause." It seemed like a very reasonable request to me, so I assured them that I would certainly give them my best educated guess at the end of that first session.

Most of the time, the ugly stories men and women quickly told me, the disrespect with which they treated each other, the length of time that they'd been in their conflicted state, and the hostility that spiked forth from both partners moved me rapidly toward pessimism rather than optimism. I ventured, to myself, that they too would clearly see and hear the blatant negativity. As the session drew to a close, I would bring the conversation back to their earlier request and say, "You asked earlier for my opinion about whether this marriage could be saved, and if you still are interested, I can tell you what I think."

"Yes," they would inevitably respond, they did want my opinion. I then stated the obvious, but gently. "There is so much anger between the two of you, and there has been for such a long period of time, that I think reestablishing harmony and good communication would be almost impossible, even with lengthy couple counseling."

Their response? Shock, outrage, and total disbelief. "What? How can you say that? We love each other. We have children. We've been together for eight years. How can you dismiss all those factors? How can you come to that conclusion after only talking to us for an hour? You're so negative. What kind of a pessimist are you? We're going to find a therapist who has faith in marriage, who believes in us!" and out the door they'd storm. The good news was that the couple was in agreement, probably for the first time in a long while, about something. The bad news was that what they were in agreement about was that I was a lousy psychologist!

After this happened four or five times, with the same general outcome, I began to wonder what I was doing wrong. I was giving the couple what they said they wanted and needed, but by their response it was obvious that they wanted something different. Even though they said very directly that what they wanted was my honest opinion, I concluded that they really wanted hope for their future, or time to come to grips with their situation, or a positive plan that they could at least work on. They did not want the stark reality that I saw and spoke of thrust upon them.

I slowly realized that it was my job to figure out a way to deliver hope and time to them, without being dishonest, manipulative, or selling my soul. So I learned to say, most of the time but not always, something like this: "I see some strengths in your relationship—parenting is important to you both, you enjoy working on your house, and you have some shared values about life and love. Certainly there are obstacles that seem to be getting in your way of living together as happily as you'd like. At this point, I would guess that overcoming these obstacles is possible, if both of you want to and have the energy to do so. Reconstructing a relationship, even with help, is a lot of work. People can tire of it before the job is done. You probably know each other better than I do and are better judges of your motivation and perseverance. I'd suggest that you discuss this further between yourselves tonight and then let me know what you decide to do."

Everything I said was true, yet I gave them what they wanted and needed—some time and some hope. I also gave them what they may not have wanted, but should have—the awareness that they knew better than I whether there was reason to believe their relationship could work.

That early experience with couples generated my first illumination about indirect influence, and the use of the technique that I later called Acting in Accord. Acting in Accord means to give people what they want and need from you, if you can, rather than communicating discordantly, withholding from them, or disagreeing with them.

Acting in Accord: What Does It Look and Sound Like?

When the target person says to you, "I think I'd prefer to work on the lunch committee rather than the program committee for the company anniversary celebration event," say, "That's fine with me," or "Great, I'd like you to find someone to switch with, if you can, so we don't short the program committee." In this case, you are assuming that he has a good reason to change, that you don't have to know what it is or evaluate the "correctness" of his choice, but just to give him what he wants and needs. If you instead act in discord you would say, "Why did you change your mind?" or "We already have too many people on the lunch committee," or "It's too late to change now." Generally, it doesn't make much difference one way or another. If you give someone what they want, they're more apt to produce than if you deny them, particularly if the denial seems arbitrary.

Tom, the sales manager for a new housing development, prides himself on Acting in Accord with customers, although he recognizes the almost innate tendency he has to withhold from someone who clearly is needy. Recently, a couple in their fifties came in to look at the models. Tim seemed quiet and reserved, while his wife, Louisa, was the talkative one, asking and telling. To Tom, attempting to read the interaction between the two, Tim seemed almost embarrassed by his wife's assertiveness compared to his own apparent nonassertiveness, but still took no action. Tom decided that Tim really wanted and needed to be treated as a person of power, even though in this situation he looked and sounded like a person of no power. So, Acting in Accord, Tom directed much of his conversation to Tim, carefully taking notes on his yellow pad, asking about his priorities, and treating him with great respect. Tom didn't ignore Louisa, but he did pay more attention to Tim. Amazingly, as Tom, a powerful-looking and acting manager, continued to treat Tim as a person with power, his wife began to treat her husband more respectfully as well. Some Modeling took place as well as Acting in Accord. Tim became more assertive, and over time became the primary decision maker on the sale.

For managers coaching less-experienced employees, teaching them Acting in Accord is an excellent early lesson in handling criticism from clients. A new hire, twenty-three-year-old Sarita, had just received feedback from her client. "This marketing piece is not at all what I wanted. I don't like the spin you put on it. You shouldn't have used the data from Europe because it's misleading. You should only use the data from Asia—and the complete data, not just a part." The natural response for this young woman, who had worked long and hard to make the piece fit exactly what she thought the customer wanted, was to become defensive and explain and justify her decisions.

Thanks to the delayed response allowed by receiving e-mail criticism rather than telephone communication, Sarita had a chance to talk to her manager, who suggested directly that she use an indirect influence technique. Specifically, he recognized that the customer was already resistant, and that the best thing to do was to tell her that she will get what she wants and needs—and mean it, without apology or excuse. He demonstrated the Acting in Accord dialogue, and role-played the suggested return phone call. "I did misunderstand what you wanted, but I have a clear picture after reading your e-mail and I'll deliver what you want on Friday." That's it.

In a management situation, when a team member says to you, in response to nothing you've said, that she spent the whole weekend working on the integration project, coming in both Saturday and Sunday, what she probably wants is acknowledgment or appreciation. The normal managerial response might be to ignore the comment, or to make some withholding or discordant remark such as "You should be able to get your work done during the regular workweek, Stone. If you can't, we may have to reevaluate your fit for this project." Or, "Get a life, Stone." Or, "Well, if you choose to spend your life at the office, that's not my problem."

If instead, you've read her well, recognized her need, and decided to use Acting in Accord, all you have to say is "I appreciate all the time you're putting in, Stone." Or, "Thanks for your hard work." When you give people what they want and need from you, the likelihood increases that they will give you what you want and need from them. This whole reciprocal process may not take place consciously, but it happens. Robert Cialdini calls it the "rule for reciprocity" in his book *Influence*. The rule says we should try to repay in kind what another person has provided us. We are obliged to repay the favor, whether or not it's stated or asked for, or even mentioned.[1]

You can use Acting in Accord effectively with a group as well as with an individual. If you, as CEO, know what outcome you want—for example, to move the company headquarters to a new, but less expensive building—and you know that the rest of your staff is against the move, you have several choices. The direct approach would be to say, "I understand your concerns, but as the CEO, I'm going to exert the privilege of the position and say we move." This is clearly a direct influence attempt, which will work to make the move happen, but in the long run will generate resistance from your staff. In a slight variation of Acting in Accord, you might ask for group input, even if you already know what they'll say, and then suggest the group look at the advantages and disadvantages of staying where you are or moving. Without demonstrating your bias, even though they may already know it, you walk the group through the advantages and disadvantages of both alternatives, guiding them in problem solving, not leading them to the conclusion you want. If you really are right, by the time they wade, unfettered, through the facts, they realize themselves that staying put isn't the best plan. They then choose to Act in Accord with you because you didn't act in discord with them. You're then in a much better position than had you used the command-and-control style.

Reading the Target Person

Clearly, the most important prerequisite for successful use of Acting in Accord is Step 2 of "The Drill" delineated in Chapter 2: reading the other person to determine what she really wants and needs from you, regardless of what she says she wants and needs, or what you might assume she wants and needs. If you can understand her position, and adapt to it, you'll undoubtedly increase the likelihood of effectively influencing her.

A recent article in *Psychotherapy* titled " 'OK, I'm Here, but I'm Not Talking!': Psychotherapy with the Reluctant Male," addressed the issue of reading the resistant male client in therapy, and giving him what he wants and needs instead of giving him what he clearly doesn't want. Research demonstrates that men in general are typically reluctant to acknowledge problems, particularly of an emotional nature. They're often uncomfortable with intimacy, as well as inexperienced with and resistant to talking about feelings—the mode of most therapeutic schools. In order to build an alliance with this kind of client, the therapist has to change her normal mode, use different guidelines, and Act in Accord instead of acting in discord and forcing the client to follow the rules of therapy. The alliance is built carefully and slowly, by conversing in the language of the client instead of in the language of therapy.

The author, J. J. Shay, rightly suggests that therapists shouldn't ask this man to play a game he didn't really choose, on a field he doesn't know, with a captain he does not yet respect, in a language he doesn't speak. Instead, the therapist needs to be low-key and nonpressuring, operating from the assumption that the reluctant patient always has a good reason to be so. He suggests showing respect for this reluctance. "You don't have to do anything you don't want to, talk about anything you prefer not to, or even continue with therapy right now." A piece of Paradox here tied with Acting in Accord can also work. "There's no rush, why don't you get back to me when your schedule is freer." Shay says, "To deal with reluctance, sit beside it."[2] Sounds like Acting in Accord to me!

Being more of a direct communicator, by virtue of personality and early assertiveness training, I made the assumption years ago that if people did tell or ask for what they wanted, then they meant what they said. This issue became the focus of my second book, *Say What You Mean, Get What You Want*. Subsequently, I discovered that many times people don't ask for what they want and need directly because they themselves may not know what they want. Or they may say directly what they want, but it is not what they really want, because they don't know that they don't know what they really want. Perhaps they do know what they want, but are too uncomfortable or too embarrassed to ask for it directly, or perhaps they have a hidden agenda and don't want you to know what they really want. Consequently, the manager has to make an educated guess, depending on his knowledge of the person and the situation, whether the person is asking for what she really wants, if there is something else she wants as well, or if there is something else she wants instead. You are of course not a mind reader, but you can develop some hypotheses about what the person wants and needs from you, and then act on them.

The goal of reading the other person is not winning a contest where you one-up someone with your superior knowledge of her inner self. For example, "You're saying that what you want is for me to provide more structure in your assigned projects, but really what you want is more approval from me in a day-to-day way." Instead, you should just use the information internally to make a choice about what technique you're going to use to influence her.

A strange phenomenon that goes along with recognizing what someone wants and needs is a judgment that, if he didn't ask for it directly, you shouldn't give it to him, or he shouldn't get it! (Inner dialogue: "I'm not going to give you approval because you shouldn't need so much anyway, and if you do, you should tell me directly instead of my having to guess, so I'm going to punish you by withholding approval from you even more than I would normally because you want it so much!") Maybe there's a stereotype operating that people who aren't direct don't deserve to get what they want. Or a principle that giving people what they want and need is losing the game and puts you in the one-down position. Any of these reactions may be less conscious, and more reflexive, but it should be noticed and managed. Otherwise, it will get in the way of your using Acting in Accord effectively.

Smart managers recognize that giving someone what she wants and needs from you, if you can do so reasonably and without selling your soul, is an extremely powerful way to influence her to give you what you want and need from her. Many times we, as managers and potential influencers, want what we want on general competitive principles, but not for a solid reason. We become oppositional to the person we are trying to influence, not "giving in" to his wishes even if his actual want is easy for us to grant. "I won't if I have to, even if I want to" can be the kind of internal dialogue that goes on. That's unproductive and unsophisticated behavior on the part of leaders.

The Case

Overcoming resistance is a big part of the job for sales professionals. They may not think in terms of dealing with resistance, but instead in terms of handling objections—a form of resistance to the product, the service, or the salesperson. It's difficult enough when the objections are to price, value, or quality, but even tougher when the customer's objections are, or seem like they are, to the individual, to salespeople in general, or even to specific categories of salespeople (such as car salespeople) in particular.

Recently, a participant in a workshop I was presenting said that she thought the most difficult customer to sell, or even begin to establish rapport with, was the "new" professional woman in her thirties or forties, who comes into the automobile dealership at lunchtime or right after work, shopping for a car and carrying a big chip on her shoulder.

Let's look at one specific example. A woman in a business suit arrives, parks her car (a 1997 Honda), and hurriedly enters the empty showroom of the Infiniti dealer. The salesperson on the floor at the time is Yustaf. He is experienced and successful, but nonetheless feels slightly uncomfortable about this woman, who looks hostile and aloof and telegraphs, "Leave me alone."

She looks around quickly at the models on the floor, scans the written brochure, and carries it with her as she returns to one of the cars she had looked over previously, an SUV—an expensive vehicle. Yustaf has headed in her direction several times, but she seems to almost purposefully change directions and move or find a different focus as he approaches. They have not made eye or voice contact.

Yustaf realizes that his usual approach—to offer his hand,

introduce himself, ask the customer her name and determine her needs—will probably not work in this situation, because she seems inaccessible at the moment. He doesn't know what to do, but knows that if he doesn't do something, she will be out the door, and perhaps not return. He will have no opportunity to even try a beginning influence attempt.

The Drill

Let's use "The Drill" here to determine what influence approach would work best.

■ *Decide what you want as an outcome of the communication.* Very simple. Yustaf wants to sell her a car. But he already senses that she is not going to buy a car from him today, or at least not now. He recognizes that he needs to break his own sales wants down into smaller segments. Right now all he wants is to establish some early rapport with her, so when she is ready to buy a car, there's a probability that she'll return to talk more to him about her purchase.

■ *Read the other person in the current situation.* Not so simple. But Yustaf does have the self-awareness to recognize that he's uncomfortable, that he generally doesn't do well with aloof, seemingly hostile women, and that he needs to figure out what to do rather than just act impulsively or use the standard "same old" approach. He really doesn't know what she wants and needs from him, but his assumption, based on his observation, is that she wants nothing—absolutely nothing. Still, as he rethinks his observations he recognizes that she must want something, even if only to gather some information. Her manner, her hurriedness, her apparent avoidance of him, her very businesslike manner, point to some other possibilities:

■ She wants some information, in a hurry, about a specific car, or about Infiniti in general.

103

- She wants any salesperson to see that she doesn't want to buy now.
- She doesn't want to be "pitched" right now.
- She doesn't want to waste time unnecessarily.
- She seems on the defensive, maybe as concerned about being intimidated by an aggressive sales approach as Yustaf is by her unfriendly manner.
- She may want recognition that she is important to this dealership and that she will be taken seriously as a customer.
- She may want to convey that she is different from most customers, particularly the stereotypical female customer, which she may think is perceived as an "easy target" by automobile salespeople.

In this situation, she has all the power, because Yustaf doesn't really know what she wants and needs. Only she knows fully what she wants and needs, and she doesn't want to give it to him, at least not now. She appears to be a resistant or oppositional customer.

Yustaf is skilled in communication skills and somewhat needy at the moment. He hasn't reached his monthly quota. He recognizes the validity of the message in Kerry Johnson's tape, *Sales Magic*: "If you can see John Smith through John Smith's eyes you will sell John Smith what John Smith buys!" In this case, it's Jane Smith, but the principle applies.[3]

But Yustaf can delay gratification for the sale and accomplish his first want, establishing rapport. He thinks he can make a fit between their wants and needs if all she desires is quick information and some acknowledgment or recognition, or a sense of being taken seriously, and he can be patient and wait awhile for what he wants—a sale.

- *Select an influencing method and technique—direct or indirect.* An indirect approach looks like the best place to start because of what Yustaf determined about the potential customer, the timing, himself, and the situation, as well as relative power, wants, and needs. Acting in Accord is an excellent way to establish rapport. He can convey to her that he sees her as a busy, important person, who doesn't need or want help right now. He can also convey to her that he understands her and is able to adapt to her. It's relatively safe, he can do it briefly, and still convey that he is tuned in to her apparent needs. He can at least try to give her what he thinks she wants and needs instead of withholding it from her, or giving her what she apparently doesn't want—a pitch and pushiness. He knows that will not work.

■ *Implement the technique.* If he translates the influence and technique decision into action and implements Acting in Accord, Yustaf would go up to the potential customer, quickly and purposefully, but not aggressively, introduce himself, shake hands firmly, and say, "I won't take up more than three minutes of your time. You seem in a hurry this noon and it looks like you already know what you want. I don't want to slow you down, but give me a holler if you'd like a detailed printout about anything you see." She may well say, "I already have what I need." You would follow that with, "Good. I'm glad you found what you wanted. Here's my card if you'd like more information at another time."

Then Yustaf should leave her alone—not abandon the showroom floor, but also not stand and look at her, or stand talking with another salesperson, looking out over the showroom floor in a way that she might feel "watched." He should engage in purposeful activity—doing paperwork or organizing marketing materials. When she leaves, he should just say, "Thanks for taking the time to stop in. We'd like to have you as a customer when you're ready."

■ *Reward yourself.* In this circumstance, Yustaf needs to reward himself, though he didn't sell a car! He's rewarding himself for doing a good job reading the customer, not acting impulsively, retreating, or repeating a sales pitch that he knew wouldn't work.

■ *Evaluate the results.* Yustaf won't know, until or unless the customer returns, whether his indirect influence approach worked or not. But he does at least know that it didn't backfire. She didn't walk out or act more hostile and, in fact, stayed another five minutes or so, appearing to be less rushed.

Fogging

Fogging is a communication technique that was originally formulated by Manuel J. Smith and is described in his book *When I Say No, I Feel Guilty*. Although Smith viewed fogging as an assertive communication technique, I see it as an indirect influence technique, somewhat akin to Acting in Accord. When you fog, you are responding to someone's criticism of you by agreeing that there may be some truth to what he says. Your response is like a fog bank, soft and receptive rather than hard and resistant. It doesn't foster further response or retaliation. Your goal is to stop the criticism, end the conversation. Saying this directly—"I want you to stop criticizing me and I don't want to talk about this anymore"—will probably bring forth exactly what you don't want: more conversation and more criticism. The criticizer is obviously an oppositional person, or at best, resistant to you and your message, or they wouldn't be criticizing you. So you don't act in discord by disagreeing. Instead, you Act in Accord by agreeing that there may be some truth to what the person is saying. You don't agree with him or say, "You're absolutely right. I am wrong." You just acknowledge that there might be some ounce of validity to his comment.[4]

Another psychologist, David Burns, uses the term "disarming technique," to describe a good way to respond to criticism. Burns says that if you can find some small piece of the criticism with which you can agree, and do so, you readily disarm your attacker. "Regardless of how unreasonable the other person's criticisms might seem, find some grain of truth in what he or she is saying and agree with that. This is a particularly powerful tool when you feel attacked." Burns says you can shoot back, run away, or disarm, but the latter is definitely best when you just want to stop the criticism.[5]

If a coworker says, "You don't listen to me when I tell you my problems," a fogging response is "Perhaps I could be a better listener." When your boss says, "You haven't been as attentive to detail on this project as I'd like," your response is "I have been less focused than usual the last couple of days." You don't apologize, you don't make promises, you only agree that there may be some truth to what the person is saying.

I view the impact of the technique more as "taking the wind out of someone's sails," rather than disarming or fogging her, but Smith and Burns have their metaphors and I have mine. Take your pick or make up your own. As much as we don't like to acknowledge it, there usually is a grain or two of truth to others' criticism of us. Instead of reflexively defending yourself, which will only escalate the criticism and intensify your defensiveness, let it go smoothly and easily by fogging. Try it. It works!

Acting in Accord with Acting in Accord

- Acting in Accord is a very easy technique to use as a beginning foray into Beyond Assertiveness and indirect influence techniques.
- Reading your target person and determining what she wants and needs isn't so easy, but it is essential to effective use of Acting in Accord.

- Fogging is a modification of Acting in Accord that you can use as a response to criticism, rather than as an initiator of an indirect influence attempt.
- Both of these techniques are widely applicable to management, sales, group, and interpersonal influence situations. You can use them one-to-one or in a presentation, with an individual or with a group.

Notes

1. R. Cialdini, *Influence* (New York: Quill, 1984).
2. J. J. Shay, "'OK, I'm Here, but I'm Not Talking!': Psychotherapy with the Reluctant Male," *Psychotherapy* 33:3 (Fall 1996), pp. 503–513.
3. K. Johnson, *Sales Magic* (audiotape) (Chicago: Nightingale Conant, 1990).
4. See M. J. Smith, *When I Say No, I Feel Guilty* (New York: Bantam Books, 1975).
5. D. D. Burns, "Persuasion: The All-Hits, No-Misses Way to Get What You Want," *Self,* April 1981, pp. 67–71.

Chapter 7

Reframing

Old Picture, New Frame

eframing refers to changing the frame or the context in which the target person perceives events, in order to change the meaning for her. Communication always takes place in a context. When the context changes, the meaning changes, and the response to the communication changes. If the context is a medical office where you're going to hear your test results and the physician says, "I have bad news," you react with high anxiety. The exact same comment, made by the owner of a dry cleaning business when you pick up your laundry and cleaning, may result instead in a mild sense of irritation as you anticipate that your clothing isn't ready as scheduled. In other situations, the phrase "I have bad news" could be used for a humorous setup, or to describe a totally inconsequential event. The same words—a different context, a different meaning, a different response.

I first heard the concept of Reframing demonstrated as a sales training technique. I don't think the word *reframing* was ever used, but certainly the point of the sales trainer was to change the context and the meaning of the word "no," teaching potential salespeople that a different use of the word would change their behavior. Trainees in a program for door-to-door selling of groceries were told that it usually takes fifty nos to get a yes. After a morning of education and motivation, they were told to go work all afternoon and try to be the first person to get fifty nos. Whoever was back to the training facility first with fifty would win a small portable TV. Suddenly the frame changed—a "no" became a very desirable acquisition instead of a sign of rejection and failure.

Reframing is a great, even if temporary, measure to loosen and release a person's perceptual frame. When you succeed in shaking someone's insistence that X marks the spot, or Y is the only way, then moving him forward—even if not quite to the place you'd like him to move to—becomes much easier and more probable. You have to help get people's feet out of the concrete before you can even think they might move onto the grass.

Reframing is also a big part of humor, myths, fables, and fairy tales. Change the frame or context and you change the meaning. *The Ugly Duckling*, *The Little Prince*, and *Cinderella* all rely on Metaphor and Reframing to influence the reader. When you realize the ugly duckling isn't a duck at all, but a swan, he ceases to be ugly.

Reframing is inherent in the humor we derive from many jokes. Change the frame or context and change the meaning— and get a laugh. What do Alexander the Great and Smokey the Bear have in common? They have the same middle name. What is the original form of the reframed term "difficult people"? A pain in the butt!

Reframing and Therapy

In the realm of therapy, many theorists have contributed to the recognition of Reframing as a powerful influence technique. Neurolinguistic Programming's Bandler and Grinder have written an entire book titled *ReFraming*. On the first page of their book, they open with what they identify as an old Chinese Taoist story that illustrates the idea of Reframing well.

A farmer owned a horse and a plow. He was considered well-to-do by his friends. And then his horse ran away. The neighbors said, "How terrible," but the farmer said, "Maybe." Soon, the horse returned and brought two wild horses with him. The neighbors were overjoyed at the farmer's good fortune, but he said, "Maybe." The farmer's son tried to ride one of the wild horses but broke his leg in the process. The neighbors expressed their sympathy to the farmer, but he said, "Maybe." The next week, officers came to draft young men for the army. The farmer's son was rejected because of his broken leg. Neighbors said how lucky he was. But the farmer just said, "Maybe."

Bandler and Grinder add, later in their book, "What Reframing does is to say, 'Look, this external thing occurs and it elicits this response in you, so you assume that you know what the meaning is. But if you thought about it this other way, then you would have a different response.' Being able to think about things in a variety of ways builds a spectrum of understanding." Any event is only good or bad depending on the context in which you perceive it.[1]

The domain of cognitive therapy probably deserves most credit for Reframing in its original use as a therapeutic technique. In its simplest form, cognitive therapy is based on the premise that thinking differently can cause you to feel and behave differently. Everyone knows that how we react to an event is primarily determined by what and how we are thinking about the event rather than the event itself. For example, let's say you don't get a promotion that you had hoped for and someone else gets the job you wanted. If you think about it as "I didn't get the promotion because my boss doesn't like me," or "She got the job instead of me because of Affirmative Action," you will feel differently about the event than if you think, "She is better suited for the job than I am. I'll hang in there until there's a better fit for me." In this situation, the individual is Reframing an event for herself rather than Reframing a situation for someone else.

Generally, when we're Reframing for ourselves, we can find something that works smoothly, because we know ourselves well. In *Say What You Mean, Get What You Want*, I talk about Reframing (and thereby changing) what you're saying to yourself as the best way to overcome negative thinking. When you overcome your negative thinking, you can change how you see an event and behave differently. For example, if I'm worried about a presentation I'm making, I might say to myself on the way to the event, "Maybe I'm going to bomb. If I don't do a good job on this, it's the end." If instead, I reframe the event and change the context in my mind, I might say to myself, "I'm experienced. I'll handle this well." I'm then able to cope with the presentation in a confident, rather than an insecure manner.[2]

In this chapter, rather than focusing on Reframing your own internal monologue, we're emphasizing Reframing other people's thinking—changing their framework for them, so the meaning will change and their behavior will change.

One of the early cognitive therapists, Albert Ellis, author of *A Guide to Rational Living*, was and still is a master of Reframing, although he doesn't use the word to describe what he does. His emphasis is always on changing the client's internal dialogue so that she will think differently and therefore change her behavior. Ultimately, he prepared his clients to reframe their own internal dialogue. But while the clients were learning the system, Ellis did the Reframing. He could be tough.

One of the funniest, and typically Ellis, Reframing attempts was to ask people who were afraid of flying what was the worst thing that could possibly happen to them when airborne. People would recount all their worst fears: a crash landing, a plunge into the freezing Atlantic, a precipitous drop out of the sky, or a midair crash. Ellis would respond, "And then what?" Inevitably, people would respond, "I'd die." Then Ellis would ask, "And what would be the worst thing about dying?" The client would respond, "Well, I wouldn't get to see my children grow up, or my business succeed, or have grandchildren, or travel." Ellis would say, "Well, what you're saying is the worst thing that could possibly happen is that you would die. We all will die. Some sooner than later. You aren't a child. You know that death is coming, one way or another. Your fear of death is irrational because it is inevitable." He reframed death as normal and expected rather than frightening or unpredictable. He also reframed people's fear of flying as fear of death, which was irrational since it was a consequence of life for all of us. Of course, this type of reframe worked very well for some people and influenced them to give up their fear of flying. For others, it did nothing. The best reframes are designed to fit each unique individual, and Ellis's was a more global approach.[3]

Donald Meichenbaum, also a cognitive therapist and an inveterate reframer, says there's nothing in the field of psychotherapy that he can't reframe and rephrase. At a workshop for psychologists, Meichenbaum told participants about a consulting visit he had made to an American state hospital, a facility for people who were chronically and severely mentally ill. As he was running a group therapy session, two patients in the group physically attacked him. He wasn't injured, but he was certainly scared. After he quickly restored himself to normalcy, he responded to the group, "This is wonderful. The staff told me the patients here were emotionally dead, but this indignation is a sign that you're definitely not. Hang on to that intensity. It's great. It's an essential ingredient of health." Definitely a reframe, with a touch of Paradox thrown in. His goal was for the staff and the patients to begin to think that all patients had the capacity to return to health. If both believed that, they might behave differently, leading to an actual return to health.[4]

Reframing in Business

The business setting also has many opportunities for Reframing an event, in order to change the meaning, in order to change people's behavior. As a trainer, I am often asked to conduct team-building workshops. Not surprisingly, team building is requested by leaders of teams that are not functioning well together. But when teams are functioning poorly, they are often in conflict and generally aren't feeling the least bit positive about building the team. Often, if or when you try to "build the team" and get members to be more cohesive, they become more resistant. They don't want to be closer to these other people they currently dislike. One cheery, upbeat, cohesiveness-building, rah-rah day will never do it. Actually, misguided attempts to build team morale and performance often make things even worse.

Consequently, I almost never call any kind of meeting, seminar, or workshop a "team-building session" because I think the concept just generates further opposition. Instead, I call such meetings something vague and enigmatic, like "Achieving Results," "Project X," or "Task Exploration." Sometimes even a somewhat paradoxical title, like "Producing Problems," can also be used to reduce the initial resistance. With a different name for the day, the team views the session more openly and individuals have less resistance. The rename or reframe is an indirect influence attempt, subtly encouraging open-mindedness and enthusiasm, discouraging opposition, defensiveness, and resistance.

Reframing can be as simple as changing the word or

phrase that someone is using, in order to change the meaning, in order to change their behavior. Salespeople often use the word "challenge" as a way of Reframing the negative words "problem" or "obstacle"—as in, "Having our quota doubled for next year will present a challenge." If the salesperson thinks of her new, big quota as a challenge, there's something positive and exciting about it. If instead, she thinks of it as a problem or an obstacle, she may feel deterred or depressed.

However, after years of use, the "challenge" reframe may have become so trite as to be almost useless. A reframe has to have a slight note of originality, subtlety, or surprise to truly create a new meaning for the listener. Another simple example, but with more creativity and some humor, would be to talk about a bullying boss's "reign of error."

A bright manager, Tonya, was recently attempting to motivate an employee, Janna, to be more expressive of her feelings as well as her thoughts at work. In initiating the discussion, Tonya said to Janna, "I sense that you repress your feelings rather than express them." Janna quickly became defensive and responded: "That's not right. I've always thought I was very introspective and analytical. I don't like that word 'repress.'" Rather than argue, or even Act in Accord, Tonya reframed the same thought in her response, adding some Metaphor. "I think of you as having a very deep well of thoughts and feelings, of knowledge and facts, of intuition and emotions. I often hear you bring big, bountiful buckets of thoughts out of the well. I'd like to hear and see more of the *feeling* buckets brimming out of the well." Yes. There's a note of creativity and surprise that may work to encourage Janna to express her emotions. This reframe, in fact, did work without a hitch and Tonya never revisited the other "r" word.

A slightly different application of Reframing was used by Jim, CEO of Resources Plus, in his attempt to indirectly influence Karbex, described in Chapter 1. The original agenda was set up in this way:

AGENDA

PROBLEMS
    Unreliable data
    Systems not working
    Low customer satisfaction
    Costs
    Billing/payment

SOLUTIONS
    Discussion

The revised agenda was set up in this way:

AGENDA

Introduction of participants	All
Overview of today's meeting and desired outcomes	Jim
Roundtable:	
What do participants want to accomplish today?	All
How can we best achieve these outcomes?	
Resolution of service issues:	All
Increasing data dependability and accuracy	
Improving systems and processes	
Increasing customer satisfaction	
Fees	
The business relationship	
Other	
Development of action plan	All

The situation was the same, but the frame was changed from a problem and conflict focus, from a you-versus-us mentality, to a joint partnering venture to resolve service issues and take positive action.

The Case

In addition to some of the simpler applications mentioned, Reframing can also be a much more global mode of indirect influence. Rita Roberts, a manager who is designated as excellent by her employees, uses Reframing as the cornerstone of her management style and the primary source of her influence. Although she hadn't previously thought of herself as using Reframing specifically, she had recognized the advantages of indirect influence and used it in a variety of forms.

As a manager, Rita always wants to convey a "can-do" attitude and influence her staff positively. She believes that always saying yes, while giving people choices and options, works best. She sets out to get people who work both with her and with the company's clients to think in this same positive, obstacle-overcoming manner. Rita gets enjoyment out of seeing people learn and develop. She wants her staff to adopt the same "can-do" mentality that she epitomizes, so modeling is also part of her repertoire of influencing skills.

Interestingly, occasionally Rita finds the power of modeling too strong. She is at a time and place in her life where she has time, energy, and the interest to work long hours. Although she truly believes that her staff doesn't need to follow the same model of working overtime that she does, and she tells them so, they don't believe what she says. Instead they are strongly influenced by what she does. Her dilemma in this case is: how to get people *not* to do what she does in terms of time spent at work, but to do what she does in terms of the "can-do" attitude.

From the day Rita first managed this team, she continually reframed to them and for them, changing "No, because" to "Yes, if." She reframes her employees' objections, obstacles, resistance, or problems into options, opportunities, or possibilities. For example, when a customer asks if he can attend a monthly policy meeting, Rita influences her staff to answer customers by replying, "Yes, if I can get an okay from the director," or "Yes, if you're willing to join the group after dinner and during the discussion." These responses work much better than the usual reply, "No, because these meetings are not open to the public." She also models the desired behavior with employees. If one of her team members comes to her with a request—"Would it be okay if the presentation from the external consultant was delivered at the June meeting instead of the May meeting?"—she'll always say, "Yes, if . . ." Even if she wants to say, "No, that's not okay because we have already announced the presentation in our newsletter," she'll figure out a way to reframe the obstacle into an option. "Yes, if you will give a brief preview presentation at the May meeting and explain that the consultant will be providing the full presentation and final report in June."

When Rita's employees ask her to do something, or to make something happen, she never responds with "No, because it violates our policies," or "No, I don't have time right now," or "No, that's not a priority." Instead, she'll respond by saying, "Yes, if we can find a way to make it fit with prior policy," or "Yes, but we'll need to work on it first thing tomorrow morning," or "Yes, if we can deal with that issue after the conference is concluded next week."

In turn, when she, or a client, makes a request of an employee and is met with "No, because I don't have time right now," or "No, because that's not part of our responsibility in this department," she is quick to reframe their "No" into a "Yes." She might say to the employee, "Yes, we could do that for them if they could wait a week," or "Yes, we could take on that responsibility if we first check it out with the technology department." This kind of Reframing will almost always work better than a direct approach: "I want you to be more positive with our clients and think about how you 'can-do' what they want instead of why you can't do what they want." The direct comment, particularly repeated, is bound to engender resistance over time, if not immediately.

Rita gave me a great and unusual example of Reframing, demonstrating her expertise at indirect influence. What was unusual in this case was Rita's use of Reframing as a way to save somebody else from getting themselves in trouble. She had led the move to install new software for the accounting function of the department and, in her usual management style, had counted on the participation of many other people in the department to guide her. A few days after the system was up and running, one of the accounting employees came to her, obviously frustrated and angry, and said, "I have a problem with you." Before he could incriminate himself further with poor communication skills, she gently responded, "You're having a problem with the software system?"

The Drill

Using "The Drill" again, let's look a little more systematically at Rita's thinking in using the Reframing technique.

■ *Decide what you want as an outcome of the communication.* Rita knows exactly what she wants. She wants everyone in her department to be thinking, communicating, and behaving in a "can-do" way.

■ *Read the other person in the current situation.* As is true with the other indirect influence techniques, you have to know enough about a person's way of thinking and behaving so that you know what kind of reframe will fit for him. A good reframe corresponds to the conditions of a particular person's needs. It fits for him, not you. It's accurate. It makes sense. It's not deceptive. It makes as much sense, in a different way, as the thought he was locked into.

In the case of Rita's management team, Reframing "No, because . . ." into "Yes, if . . ." is valid for most people. It doesn't take away their concerns, it just turns problems and barriers into possibilities or opportunities. It's not a huge leap for most people on her team, even the ones who started out with the most negative attitudes. There are other reframes of "can't do" that might not work as well with a group or even an individual. If you reframe negativity as laziness, stubbornness, or a bad attitude, it wouldn't do the job. Even if you reframe the "can't do" as something positive—such as a strong, detailed approach to problem identification, or an ability to identify barriers to success—there may be less generalizability than what Rita chose.

Certainly, the better you know the person you're attempting to influence with Reframing, the better are your chances of making a fit. If you know someone just saw and marveled at the movie *Everest*, Reframing his long, arduous, dangerous, and almost impossible struggle to win a legal case might be to say he's "the Beck Weathers of the state criminal justice system." To someone who didn't read the book *Into Thin Air*, or see the *Everest* movie, your comment would have no meaning. You changed the context, but you didn't change her perception, or the meaning of the event, so you won't change her behavior. When your reframe doesn't work, it's usually because you haven't chosen a reframe that fits the individual in the situation. When it works, it is often because you have made a good choice of reframe based on your deep knowledge of the person. What you said, the words or phrases you used, freed her to think and behave differently.

■ *Select an influencing method and technique—direct or indirect.* Rita chose a Beyond Assertiveness approach, and specifically the indirect influencing technique of Reframing, primarily because she thought it worked best for her as a manager in terms of her philosophy of management, her belief about customer service, her own skills as a communicator, and her personality. She persisted with it because it continued to work for her and her staff.

Relying heavily on one's preferences and style as a leader is more suitable with Reframing than with any other indirect influence technique. Reframing works best when it fits the individual's way of thinking, but it relies less on an accurate read of the person than other BA techniques such as Matching or Acting in Accord. It also works well with people at different levels of resistance—from almost none to a great deal. And there are few negative consequences of a poor reframe. The worst thing that can happen is that the reframe doesn't take, and the target person stays stuck in his or her perceptual concrete and thinks you're on some weird wavelength. The influencer can try several other reframes until she finds one that does fit, without generating additional resistance.

The Spin

- Reframing can work well with an individual, a team, or a huge group.
- Using Reframing, for yourself as well as others, is fun and unleashes your latent creativity.
- Reframing the context of an event for others can be extremely freeing for them.
- Once you get the hang of it, Reframing can easily become a great tool to use with yourself and others to encourage flexibility and alter behavior.

Notes

1. R. Bandler and J. Grinder, *ReFraming* (Moab, UT: Real People Press, 1982).
2. See J. Tingley, *Say What You Mean, Get What You Want* (New York: AMACOM, 1996).
3. See A. Ellis and R. Harper, *A Guide to Rational Living* (Hollywood, CA: Wilshire Books, 1997).
4. D. Meichenbaum, telephone interview, October 8, 1997. See also D. Meichenbaum and D. Turk, *Facilitating Treatment Adherence* (New York: Plenum Press, 1987).

Chapter 8

Paradox
The Unexpected

Paradox, for the purposes of this book, is best defined as a statement that seems contradictory, contrary to common sense, unbelievable, or absurd, but may actually be true. A paradoxical communication is contrary to expectations, or to apparent logic, or even to the "right" thing to say. A recent article in *Modern Maturity*, "Rules for Aging," demonstrates a simple form of Paradox. The author, Roger Rosenblatt, says that as we get older, instead of taking positive action as we are urged to do all of our lives, we need to focus on not doing things and thinking negatively, rather than positively, about certain topics. He gives a list of "not's" and "don'ts":

- *Nothing matters.* "It does not matter . . . if you're having a bad hair day, or a no hair day; if you have spinach in your teeth or if you lose your teeth in your spinach. It doesn't matter."
- *Nobody is thinking about you.* "I promise you. Nobody

is thinking about you. They are thinking about themselves, just like you."

- *Do not go to your left.* The term "go to your left" means to strengthen your weakness. Rosenblatt says it may work for basketball, but not life: "If you attempt to strengthen a weakness, you will grow weaker."

- *Never give honest, open criticism to anyone.* "When the muse of candor whispers in your ear, swat it, take a long walk, a cold shower, and clear your head."[1]

His suggestions definitely run contrary to our expectations and experience. We would expect a motivating soul to tell us that what we do, think, or say really matters; that people around us truly care about us and see us as important; that of course we can and should strengthen our weaknesses through practice and positive mental attitude; and finally, that being open, honest, and direct is always the best way to communicate. Rosenblatt, however, is obviously being paradoxical intentionally, which definitely makes us laugh a little, think more than we would if given standard advice, and perhaps even change our behavior.

Robert Redford, as Tom Booker in the movie *The Horse Whisperer*, does a great job of using the technique of Paradox to indirectly influence thirteen-year-old Grace. She is the victim of a horrific accident that resulted in the death of a friend and injured her horse and herself, physically and psychologically. Grace's mother, Annie, has driven across the country with her to consult with a reluctant Booker about rehabilitating the injured animal. She is hoping that as the horse recovers physically and psychologically, so will Grace.

When Booker shows up at the motel to meet with Grace and her mother, Grace says to him, "In case she didn't tell you, I don't want to be a part of this, okay?" Grace is letting Booker know, up front, that she has no interest in the evaluation or possible rehabilitation of the horse. Moviegoers understand Grace's resistance and recognize that she is currently in an averse mode of thinking and behaving. Although Booker doesn't know the history of the horse and rider, he seems to understand as well.

In the next scene, Booker says firmly to Grace's mother, when she asks Grace if she'd like to go with them to the stall, "Probably best she stay behind!" He and Annie leave, after which Grace, of course, rushes to get her shoes on and follow them to the barn. Neither Grace, Booker, nor Annie says anything about her apparent change of heart. Booker's use of Paradox initiates the long path of rehabilitation for both girl and horse, a path lined with Booker's indirect influence techniques with Grace as well as the horse.

One of the most successful and risky paradoxical interventions I ever undertook was as a parent with my twelve-year-old daughter. Sara was a very bright girl who suddenly became dumb. When I went to the first parent-teacher meeting of the year, several of the teachers, who knew Sara previously, commented about the change they saw in her. Last year, she had often raised her hand, initiated topics, reported on her homework assignments. Now she rarely raised her hand, and when asked a question by a teacher she often responded, "I don't know." The teachers weren't quite sure what was going on and were surprised and confused by this dramatic change in her behavior.

I too was surprised, but not confused. Sara was going through that god-awful stage I'd read about in which young women recognize that young men don't necessarily adore brilliant young women, so they "dumb down" to become more desirable to them.

I was stunned and disappointed. As a long-standing feminist who had attempted to raise my sons and daughter with egalitarian gender values, I thought somehow or other she would be immune from this ugly symptom. Wrong. I contemplated briefly, but intensely, how to handle the situation. I decided to use an indirect influence approach. I chose Paradox.

When I returned from the meeting and Sara inevitably asked me what was discussed, I told her that the teachers had said she wasn't doing so well this year. They weren't quite sure what had happened but she didn't seem to have the answers anymore or know the homework assignments or ask intelligent questions.

I told Sara I had explained to the teachers that perhaps we had all made an error in judgment and that maybe Sara really wasn't as smart as we thought after all. I suggested that we all needed to reduce our expectations of her lest she feel insurmountable pressure to perform in ways she wasn't capable of performing. She looked at me and listened intently, but said nothing. I was sympathetic, but didn't push a discussion.

Boom. The next day her behavior changed, both at home, and as I later found out, at school too. Better yet, she never returned to the brief few months' pattern of underachievement. I never said a word to the teachers or to Sara about this paradoxical intervention. She was, of course, given positive reinforcement for her renewed "smart" behavior, but no allusions or comparisons were made to the "dumb" times. Only as I was writing this book did I tell my daughter about that indirect influence attempt. She remembered the situation clearly, and her internal response was: "I am *too* smart and I'll prove to you all that you're wrong." She laughed afterward at how effective it had been.

The normal direct response on my part in the situation with Sara would be to jump on her changed behavior and do a little motivational speech, perhaps with some guilt induction for letting down her high-expectations mom. I might have set some limits for time spent doing homework, demanded better grades for the next marking period, or said I would sit down with her and help her with her homework regularly.

My guess is that none of these techniques would have produced the same good results that the Paradox did. As a matter of fact, the direct approach would probably have added complexity, rebellion, and further undesirable consequences to the initial problem.

Paradox in Therapy

Jay Haley, a well-known therapist and follower of Milton Erickson, a pioneering psychiatrist, discusses the use of Paradox in his book *Problem-Solving Therapy*. The paradoxical directive, given by the therapist, has two levels on which two messages are communicated: "change," and within the framework of the message, "don't change." He talks about giving directives, or instructions, to clients and says there are two different ways to do so: "(1) telling people what to do when the therapist wants them to do it, and (2) telling them what to do when the therapist does *not* want them to do it—because the therapist wants them to change by rebelling." He refers to the second category as "paradoxical tasks."

Haley comments, "These tasks may seem paradoxical to family members because the therapist has told them he wants to help them change, but at the same time he is asking them not to change." For example, if an individual comes to therapy complaining that she worries too much, that she spends all day worrying, the therapist might suggest paradoxically that she worry more systematically—two hours, three times a day. When the client next comes in and says she doesn't have time to worry six hours a day, that she can only worry two hours a day and the therapist's idea was stupid, the therapist must calmly take the putdown. She does not smugly point out that worrying two hours a day is much better than eight hours a day, as the client said she was doing before, and therefore the intervention was brilliant and it worked. Whether you want to call this approach reverse psychology or Paradox, it doesn't matter. But it is clearly an indirect influence technique.

Haley suggests that the best situation in which to use this approach is with clients who like to see the therapist try and fail. This is a good description of the oppositional person. The therapist is pushing the client to improve and the client is resisting, but still goading him to keep on pushing. Very frustrating for the therapist, and it doesn't fix things.[2]

Paradox with Difficult People at Work

The same principle applies to managing people who are oppositional or difficult, even if for different reasons than with clients in therapy. Robert Bramson wrote a classic book about oppositional and other kinds of difficult people called *Coping with Difficult People*. His book, based on research with four hundred managers and employees, concluded that 10 percent of workers are troublemakers, 70 percent of employees can't cope with troublemakers, and 20 percent aren't bothered by troublemakers. Obviously, the focus needs to be on more effective coping with the troublemakers.

Bramson puts forth an interesting proposition: People who are difficult have learned to continue with their behavior because it has worked for them. They do their difficult thing and generally get the same, predictable response from others. For example, a bully will provoke a tearful response or perhaps a weak attempt to fight back. Neither of these works. The bully has learned how to manage each of those predictable responses and come out a winner. Bramson says the best way to cope with difficult people, whether they're bullies or negative people, complainers or indecisive workers, is to respond to them in a way that is different from the usual or expected.

Instead of being put off balance by their response, you put them off balance by your response.

Further, Bramson says that his suggestions might open him to the charge of being manipulative, because he tells the reader to act with purpose and forethought—to plan and to think through the best way to respond. But he insists that his coping strategies are not intended to overpower the difficult person, but instead to balance the power over time. He notes that his suggestions are ways to manage your own behavior, rather than ways to manage the other person's behavior.

Although the word is never specifically mentioned in *Coping with Difficult People*, the principles behind Paradox and some of Bramson's coping mechanisms are similar, and for similar reasons. The target person is negative, oppositional, resistant, hostile, or defensive—not a good candidate for candor and assertiveness. Instead, people should do something different from what comes naturally in communicating with the difficult person. For example, Bramson suggests being friendly with "Sherman Tanks," taking a strong, one-down position with someone who is always trying to one-up you, or not breaking the silence with someone who has "clammed up" for no apparent reason. In part, these maneuvers are great because they are unexpected. They are paradoxical. They are techniques that put other people off balance and alter the interpersonal pattern that they are expecting.[3]

My own favorite business experience with Paradox took place several years ago. I had been hired by a large international manufacturing company to transform a group of aggressive, hostile, resistant, and competitive executives into a collaborative, cooperative, cohesive work team. They knew they had negative, destructive communication—and they liked it that way!

I had been duly warned by the human resources contact person: This group kills presenters, and they're proud of it. I had been hired because no one from their HR or training department was willing to face this group of senior executives. What could I do? What should I do? Could I succeed or was the venture a foregone failure? I thought long and hard. I put hours into devising my influence strategy. I knew that direct communication would never work. They had the power. They could do a better job of directness with me than I could ever do with them. There wasn't a fit between my resources of power and their motive base of power. If I were open and honest with them, if I revealed the least bit of vulnerability, they would go for the kill. I had to use indirect influence. It was the only way.

I opened the four-hour session in this way: "I am Judy Tingley. I understand that this group kills presenters. I would like you to conclude for yourselves whether someone who would take on this task, with this group, knowing what has happened in the past, is crazy, dumb, or undeservedly egotistical or, instead, is very capable, experienced, smart, competent, and a risk taker." I had used Paradox, with a little Confusing technique thrown in, to get the outcome I wanted right off the bat.

We've focused primarily on using Paradox with people who are difficult in an active, and often aggressive, or one-up mode. It's also useful with people who are passive-aggressive—they're angry, but demonstrate it by not saying or doing anything direct—or just plain resistant to doing what we want them to do. But a paradoxical approach can also be used very effectively with nonassertive employees, or people who just don't seem to have the necessary confidence or self-esteem to do the job, and keep telling you about it.

Let's say you have a new employee, Aria, who was hired to do a specific job, requiring familiarity with some highly sophisticated software. She came into the job with some beginning knowledge of the program, but hasn't seemed to accelerate her skill at a very rapid pace. She has come to you, her manager, several times to bemoan her slowness, her lack of skill, her inability to do the job she was hired to do. You have reassured her several times, to no avail. Aria still complains, seeks frequent reassurance, and stays on the same plateau. The learning curve is going nowhere. You decide to use Paradox to jolt her out of her pattern.

The next time Aria comes to tell you about her angst and inability, instead of reassuring her, you say, "I've been giving your concern some serious thought and I'm beginning to come around to your way of thinking. You may not be able to learn this program adequately to do the job we hired you to do. Perhaps we were both fooled by the fact that you had a beginning knowledge and seemed ready to blossom into full knowledge. You do seem inordinately slow, as you mentioned, and you just haven't acquired the skill, as you know. Perhaps you're one hundred percent right."

Aria will not expect this response. She had probably eased quite comfortably into the pattern you and she have already established—she acknowledges ineptitude, you boost her up. Now, you suddenly change the pattern. She's stunned, but probably will change her pattern in response, which is what you want.

Ideally, once you've taken the initiative in confirming her lack of skill, using her own words and opinions, she will take the initiative in reassuring you that she can in fact do what needs to be done. Aria's response might be, "Well, I do have the basic knowledge and I really think I can get it down pat within the next month if I gear up a little more." But instead of encouraging her at this point, still stay paradoxical and express some ongoing doubt. "I'm not so sure, but maybe it's possible. I have my doubts after three months." Again, Aria will probably come back and reassure you even more vehemently. "I know I can do it. Just give me a little more time. I'll get it." You conclude the meeting with an enigmatic "We'll see."

By using Paradox, you provide an opportunity for Aria

to mobilize her resources to get the job done. If she does, then you're both in good shape. If she can't, then you find out more quickly than by repeating the old pattern ad infinitum, and you get someone else to take over her job.

When I suggest this response to managers, they often gasp and say, "I couldn't do that. It's cruel." From my perspective, you are actually doing the employee a favor. You've not succeeded with your directness, nor has she. Your reassurance has enabled her to stay where she is. If things don't change, however, ultimately she'll lose her job. Giving her an opportunity to step up to the plate by agreeing with, and even escalating, her negative self-evaluation, is the kindest thing you can do to save her from herself and from you—if she is rescuable. If she's not, you'll both find out faster.

The Case

Mary Cook was a construction foreman in charge of her own crew. The man with whom she worked, Danny, younger than she, but of equal status and with his own crew, seemed bothered by the fact that a woman dared to even be there on a construction site. She was the only woman. He was twenty-four, she was forty. Although he had no authority relative to her, he often commented to her about her job, her crew, her work, her actions, and her appearance.

Danny was a screamer, a dominant, aggressive crew chief. Mary was a quiet, collaborative crew chief. She had made an independent decision to hand out paychecks at noon on Fridays for her crew, because that's what they said they preferred. Handing the checks out at noon, instead of at the end of the day, was a new practice. Danny angrily told her she couldn't do that. It wasn't the way they did things and, if she changed things for her crew, it would put pressure on everyone else to make the same change for their crew. He told her that the other guys weren't going to change, they liked things the way they were, so she'd have to go back to the old way.

At this point, let's bring in "The Drill," to help figure out how Mary could best handle this situation.

The Drill

■ *Decide what you want as an outcome of the communication.* This was not a complex decision. Mary very simply wanted Danny to leave her alone, to get out of her business as a crew chief, and to stop acting as if he were her boss. She wanted to influence him to bug off and let her continue to give her crew their checks on Fridays at noon. ·

■ *Read the other person in the current situation.* It was clear to Mary that Danny was very traditional in his approach to his work, the construction industry, and probably life in general. From his perspective, she wasn't part of that tradition. He probably wanted to get rid of her just as much as she wanted to get rid of him. One of the differences between the two— something Mary saw and knew she could use effectively— was her maturity and experience, versus his immaturity. She also knew she could be more patient, calmer, and less impulsive than Danny. She had better self-management skills.

Mary also recognized that the best time was right now, while the screaming was going on. There was nothing to be gained by her waiting until Danny was calm. As a matter of fact, his agitation was useful to her. It strengthened her position.

■ *Select an influencing method and technique—direct or indirect.* Mary knew immediately that she'd never beat Danny at his own game. He would always be better than she at the aggressive, screaming, yelling, direct, put-down approach. She remembered a poster she'd seen on the wall of someone's office. It applied perfectly to this situation. "Never mud wrestle with a pig. You get muddy and the pig likes it." She was very happy to avoid the mud wrestling and decided to use an indirect approach instead. Mary realized that if she acted in a totally unexpected way with Danny, instead of getting into what she called "uproar," she might finally be successful at influencing him to leave her alone. Although she didn't make a conscious decision at the time to use Paradox, because she didn't know about it, that's exactly what she did.

■ *Implement the technique.* Let's go back briefly to where we were in the interaction between Danny and Mary, before we moved into "The Drill." He told her that "the other guys weren't going to change, they liked things the way they were, so she'd have to go back to the old way." The louder and more vehement Danny became, the more quietly Mary spoke. The more irate he became, the more calmly she acted. But Mary was not going to change her decision. She wanted to say, "Drop dead," and "Get out of my face," but she didn't. Finally, when he screamed at her, "You don't know shit about our traditions in the construction business! You don't belong," Mary responded quietly, "Whatever made you believe I was a traditional person? Do I look like a traditional person? Do I talk like a traditional person? Do I act like a traditional person?" Mary's statement capped her overall paradoxical response to Danny: staying calm, not hostile, being quiet in contrast to his yelling, avoiding the counterattack, and finally pointing indirectly to his lack of logic. Danny was rendered speechless. He turned and walked out.

Mary's indirect influence attempt worked. The guy never spoke to her again and, within a few months, he left the job. Mary didn't get muddy and Danny didn't like the wrestling, because Mary never went in the mud! Her use of Paradox was probably the best approach Mary could have used to get what she wanted.

Important Points to Forget

- Paradox seems highly risky at first to the beginning indirect influencer.
- If you're feeling hostile and combative, don't try Paradox. It won't have the desired effect. You have to be calm and brave to pull it off.
- Aggressive, passive-aggressive, and nonassertive employees all make good potential targets for Paradox.
- Never admit or acknowledge what you're attempting to accomplish with Paradox. Doing so will eliminate it as a tool in your influence box for that person in the future. You'll take away the surprise factor.

Notes

1. R. Rosenblatt, "Rules for Aging," *Modern Maturity*, May–June 1999, p. 22.
2. J. Haley, *Problem-Solving Therapy* (New York: Harper and Row, 1978).
3. See R. Bramson, *Coping with Difficult People* (Garden City, NY: Anchor Press/Doubleday, 1981).

Chapter 9

Confusing

A Disarming Approach

onfusing is an indirect influence technique that originally comes from the communication lingo of hypnosis. When you speak to people in a somewhat confusing, rambling manner, their tendency is to turn you off, stop listening, go inside their minds, and think things through in their own way, while you're still Confusing them. This form of indirect influence is particularly useful when you want people to take more initiative, to be more independent, but don't want to tell them to be that way directly. It's an easy technique to use and fun to implement. The main barrier for you as a manager may be that you pride yourself on being an excellent, clear communicator. When you lapse into the Confusing technique, you do risk losing that reputation, if infrequently. The reward comes when the outcome you want is achieved.

Confusing and Therapy

Confusing is an indirect influence technique that I began using in my early therapist days, when I was learning about hypnosis. When you are using hypnotic language in therapy, you are attempting to influence someone to stay in a slightly altered state of consciousness—a state similar to one we all experience fairly regularly. You know the feeling. You're staring out the window, thinking of nothing, or everything. If someone interrupts you and asks how long you've been sitting there or what you were thinking about, you have almost no idea. You're in an altered state of consciousness. You're not asleep. You're not unconscious. You're just there, but not there. You're very absorbed in one experience, the altered-state experience, and totally distracted from another—the reality, here-and-now, experience.

One of the ways a therapist influences people to stay in a slightly altered state is to use the Confusing technique. You might say to them, "Maybe you'll remember what I said or maybe you'll forget, and it really doesn't matter because we're all forgetting things at some time and remembering them at others. And, of course, we don't really forget things, they just move backward someplace behind or in front of things that we've already forgotten to remember or remembered to forget. Sometimes we remember things we'd rather forget and other times we forget things we'd rather remember, but remembering and forgetting are all parts of the same process and it's not really important." By the time the therapist finishes this soliloquy, any target person would be thinking his own thoughts, hearing his own words, seeing his own pictures. He is completely distracted from what the therapist is saying and instead is absorbed in his own thoughts.

When I began working as a therapist, I recognized an important limitation in my skills. I was very good with people who were similar to me—left-brained, direct, logical, primarily cognitive problem solvers. A direct approach often worked well with them. I could use the principles of cognitive therapy, employ a problem-solving approach, set goals, and develop an action plan. We would usually be successful.

However, I wasn't so great with people who were right-brained, more emotionally expressive, inarticulate, or "arty," because a direct, left-brained approach didn't work so well with them. In an effort to find how I could influence this type of client more effectively, I not only put a flip chart and felt-tipped markers in my office, so I could draw pictures, but I also decided to expose myself to more right-brained approaches to therapy—Gestalt therapy, Ericksonian therapy, and hypnosis. Although I never became a complete convert to any of these styles, I did become more eclectic as I embraced bits and pieces from them all.

The Confusing technique is one of those embraceable bits. I've continued to use this indirect influence technique in individual and group therapy, as well as with individual coaching clients, and with groups in the business setting.

Confusing and Business

I used the Confusing technique as part of a wholesale Beyond Assertiveness approach that I applied with a very resistant group of senior male managers. This is the same group that said they "killed presenters" which I described earlier in Chapter 8. The group, in feedback they sent from a preparatory task I had given them, said they were a results-oriented, butt-busting, make-it-happen group.

In an effort to get their buy-in, I started out, after using Paradox, by saying, "I understand from your feedback to me that you are a very results-oriented group. Once you decide what you want, you make it happen. So it seems to me the first thing you need to decide today is, exactly what is it you want to accomplish? When you decide, you can then go after the result. If you want to change the negative, hostile behavior that you've said is a frequent and bothersome barrier in this group, then I'm sure you can do it, and probably in less than the four hours we have allotted. If you decide you don't want to do it, then I'm sure you can accomplish that as well, but it will probably take you longer than four hours to get what you want."

There was silence. They group looked somewhat adrift, an unlikely appearance for these highly focused, intense individuals. I had confused them, briefly perhaps, but nonetheless effectively. So now they either had to go deep inside and attempt to figure out this Confusing message—or just go along with me.

Attempting to figure the message out would lead to further Confusion. You can imagine the questions that might wander through their minds:

- "I want to demonstrate that we're results-oriented, but then I'm giving in to her."
- "I don't really want to change this behavior, but I sure don't want to be here longer than four hours."
- "What is she talking about?"
- "If we do it in less than four hours, then we'll have to give up some of that negative, hostile behavior that we all know and love. We'll have to change. No way."
- "If we want to hang on to that great, familiar, negative, obstructive behavior, we'll have to spend the day here. No way."

Basically, there could have been many more thought possibilities resulting from my brief, Confusing comments to them. But it worked. They were all off somewhere in their heads, rather than focusing all their attention on locking horns with me, and I was right there, moving forward with no opposition.

As a manager, when you choose to use the Confusing technique, you as the speaker are influencing the listener to come up with her own answer or solution to a problem, her own vision or plan, her own idea or creative thought about a situation. Using the Confusing technique also provides your employees with the opportunity to indirectly one-up you. Because you are occasionally being Confusing, they can easily add an idea to what you said to improve on your thought, without appearing to challenge or compete with you. When a leader uses Confusing, the other person goes inside his own head, to avoid being confused by the leader's rambling. The employee can come up with a brilliant idea that seems on the surface to be totally disconnected from the manager's thinking. Therefore, he can more readily risk being innovative without fearing to seem critical.

Letitia is a manager who has been busy micromanaging her team. Her boss, Rudy, in her performance appraisal, was critical of this aspect of her management, citing too much hand-holding, positive reinforcement, and time spent with employees meeting, encouraging, teaching, coaching, and even doing their work for them. Rudy thought Letitia was enabling her staff to stay put, to become overdependent on her, and to stop developing their skills. He said he didn't care how she did it, but she needed to start pushing her staff to become more innovative, independent, and self-starting. She agreed. And she decided to use indirect influence to accomplish that goal because she knew a direct approach would foster resistance—and it didn't fit her own comfort level.

Here's what Letitia, using the Confusing approach at a staff meeting, might sound like:

Letitia (*manager*): "Okay, we need to revisit our priorities today. We have so much to do, and so many deadlines, and too many deliverables, in too short a time. Let's start by talking about who's primarily responsible for what. Maria and Loretta are in charge of the strategic directions with some help from Helga and Morris, who are still primarily responsible for the Men's Sales Initiative, but also secondaries for the evaluation of 360-degree feedback evaluation programs, which Sidney and Sigrun are first in line for, but also have accountability for the new software search."

Matt: "You didn't mention me or Patricia in that lineup, unless I missed it. We're first in line on the recruitment project, which I thought was the highest priority for our company overall, even though it doesn't have a deadline. Then we're secondary for the 360-degree feedback evaluation program."

Maria: "Let's get this written down in chart or table format, so it's not so confusing and we're sure we've covered everything. Letitia, why don't you write that all down on the whiteboard or the flip chart so it's clear."

Letitia (*stays seated*): "The two M's here, Matt and Maria, sound like they've got some concern about whether all this data is complete and accurate. How about the third M on this team, Morris? Do you think the same thing, or are you thinking something completely different from the other M's?"

Morris: "Well, I'm not sure what you mean, but I think Maria's idea is a good one so we're sure we're all on the same page. I don't mind putting it in table form on the whiteboard and then doing it on the computer and giving everyone a copy later today."

Letitia (*makes no comment, nor makes any move*)

Maria: "Morris, let me put it up on the flip chart, if you don't mind, because I have a clear idea of how it would work best. Then you can just rip off the sheet and take it back to your cubicle with you to do the table on the computer."

Yes, this indirect influence approach by Letitia does and will take longer than a direct approach. It will be almost a culture change for this group. But using the Confusing technique, as well as other indirect influence approaches, will almost definitely work better with this team than other possible direct approaches such as:

Letitia: "I've been with this team now for six months and I've tried to be a very supportive manager. But now it's time for all of you to start being more independent, creative, and participative—so I'm going to be spending less time with you, providing less guidance and structure, and counting on all of you to step on the accelerator and get into self-start gear."

Or:

Letitia: "I just had a performance appraisal, and Rudy said I'm too good to you guys. He told me I had to stop pampering you all so much because I had other things I wasn't paying attention to while I'm micromanaging all of you. So, be prepared. You're going to be on your own because I've got to get with it here and do what he says, or I'm in trouble. Starting now."

We could come up with three or four variations, but they would all have something in common. They would inevitably generate some hostility, resistance, and reluctance, or even opposition on the part of Letitia's staff because, to them, she would be going from being a good guy to a bad guy, and no one likes that, whatever the reason might be. Instead, she'll be moving them slowly but comfortably toward independence if she continues to use the Beyond Assertiveness approach.

The Case

Suzanne is the executive director of a not-for-profit organization. She is smart, capable, experienced, and politically astute.

She rescued the organization from two years without a director and from a board that was policy-driven but not budget-minded or operations-savvy. The directors were more into the social aspects of their volunteerism, planning events, but not keyed into fund-raising in a general sense. Suzanne was viewed as the savior when she came on board. Everyone on the board breathed a huge sigh of relief, and essentially became even less involved, at least for her first year as ED.

The second year, a new activist board chair set up committees that forced more involvement from the board members—a budget committee, a fund-raising committee, a procedures and policies committee, a special events group, a board development group, and a program committee. Consequently, people became more active and involved with the organization. Suzanne began to encounter more questions about exactly what she was doing, what the organization was doing, who was their target market, how were they evaluating outcomes, what were the underlying principles of the program, and other similarly sticky concerns that the directors knew nothing about. Somewhat suddenly, board members wanted a lot of information, stood in line to visit program sites, attend programs, meet the clients, view the curriculum, and talk to the staff.

Anyone in Suzanne's position would probably be taken aback by the quick shift. She had been left alone to do her own thing for more than a year. Now, board members seemed to be questioning her judgment, her work, and the program. Furthermore, board members were around all the time, observing, asking, checking, and monitoring, after having been almost totally absent before. Suzanne became more visibly stressed, less amiable, and, most important, more talkative.

Whether she initially made a choice to confuse the board or not, my guess is that she found what she was doing, Confusing board members with her whirlwind of words, resulted in directors backing off. She then purposely continued using the Confusing technique because it worked to increase her autonomy. Here's what a Confusing indirect influence attempt from Suzanne might sound like:

Zillith (*board member*): "Suzanne, I need to find out how to get a list of the enrollees in our program for the last year. We want to obtain some feedback from them about the program, now that they've been out in the real world for a while. We'd like to find out what suggestions they might have for improvement. Of course, I'll send you a proposal before implementing any survey, but I would like to get started on collecting names, addresses, and phone numbers so we at least have some idea about how many people are available."

Suzanne: "Well, that's not as easy as you'd expect. The Dawson grant doesn't provide for a good data collection method for our participants, and although the Exodus software isn't so bad, it *is* old. As you know, with the newer Thompson funds available to us we can upgrade, and the technology to dictate better methods will be available as soon as that grant comes through, but in the meantime with the loss of the city funding, we can't take chances that the Department of Social Services will let us use their hardware or software to gather information. Then there's always the problem, of course, of the reliability of the data. It was originally collected at one time, when the participants left our program, and of course now we're trying to collect it at another time, so conceivably what was true a year ago is no longer true and we have invalid data. You could be spending a lot of time trying to locate people who can't be located.

"That's an internal as well as an external problem as you might guess, and an obstacle to our doing solid follow-up, but until we recover the fifty thousand dollars we lost through the integration of the city, county, and state funds, it's difficult to determine exactly who and where our participants are, where they came from, and where they're going.

"Then again, you have to look at the validity of that kind of feedback anyway. Gathering outcome information isn't a requirement of most of our funding sources and perhaps that isn't the best way to use your time, my time, or the board's time. Maybe the board is better off dealing with policy issues, rather than the internal workings here of the organization, but of course that's really a board position, in terms of how you see the role of the board, and not mine. But I see my role, and that of the program director, as being primarily and exclusively responsible for the integrity of the program.

"Carlos, the program director, certainly wouldn't set up a program that he didn't think was good, and that wasn't acceptable by national standards. Are you familiar with the benchmarking study that was conducted on best practices several years ago by the national organization? They found that evaluation studies were a waste of time and that the local organizations were more effective if they focused on fundraising and grant writing rather than spending a lot of time focusing on a program that had been in place for several years, and seemed to be working well."

Zillith: (*At this point, Zillith has turned off and is staring blankly into space, thinking only, "How can I get out of here?" She has forgotten her simple question: "How can I find the names, addresses, and phone numbers of program participants in the last year?" She is confused, bored, overwhelmed, feeling somewhat uninformed about the true workings of the organization, in over her head, and perhaps out of line in her role as a board member. She just wants out of the conversation for now.*) "Thanks for your time, Suzanne. You certainly know a lot about how this organization works."

Are any readers suddenly aware of someone using this BA technique with them? It's not what I'd call the best and highest use of the Confusing technique, but it certainly is effective.

The Drill

As usual, let's use "The Drill" to analyze this conversation and the use of the Confusing technique. Unlike many of the other indirect influence techniques, the decision to use the Confusing technique relies more on the manager and the fit of needs, or lack of fit, between the manager and his or her employees than it does on reading individual target people.

■ *Decide what you want as an outcome of the communication.* In this use of Confusing, Suzanne wanted to gain autonomy in the work situation by diluting the intensity of board members' motivation to be closely involved with the internal workings of the organization.

■ *Read the other person in the current situation.* Suzanne doesn't necessarily know all, or even some, of the board members particularly well, but she does know the history of the board. The board members have changed little since she was hired as executive director, although the makeup of the executive committee has changed considerably. Historically, the board was more of a hands-off group that had a social status to it and a yearly fun fund-raising event that was the focus of the members' energy and time. There had been little board training, no board retreat to talk about strategic planning for the future, little participation by board members in or at programs, no involvement of members with clients, and inconsistent attendance at board meetings. In the past, the ED, or acting ED, had been pretty much on his or her own to run the show. Suzanne had gone after the job and accepted the job as ED with the expectation that she would continue in that same path, unfettered by the board.

Suzanne thought, as she read the board, that although a new, apparently activist group had sprung up out of nowhere, they might easily be influenced to return to their former position as social fund-raisers, with little interest in the inner workings of the organization.

■ *Select an influencing method and technique—direct or indirect.* Suzanne chose an indirect influence technique primarily because a direct technique seemed risky. She didn't want to do it, it probably would generate renewed energy and motivation for board involvement, and she could always try it later if the indirect didn't work. To try to influence the board members directly would sound like this:

Suzanne: "I took this job with the expectation that the board was a hands-off board. I've made plans, hired staff, developed goals that all go along with that expectation. Now that it appears that a small subgroup is getting active and wanting to be very involved with the internal workings of our organization, it's really getting in the way of our operating effectively. We are having to spend much more time meeting with board members, answering questions, preparing reports, explaining programs, and talking about outcomes than we ever have in the past. That takes time away from our jobs, our mission, and our goals. We would prefer that you go back to the way you were and, further, that you select new board members based on their interest in the previous way of doing things rather than the present way."

Could that be done? Yes, but in the paradoxical response to life that some of us unwittingly create, resentment, hostility, and opposition could and probably would result. Ultimately, the board has the power to hire and fire an executive director. It's a chance that Suzanne wasn't willing to take. Because she had accepted the position with a belief that the ED and board were distinct, separate, and not highly interdependent, she preferred to attempt to return people, positions, and politics back to their original mindset. She did so with Confusing.

■ *Implement the technique.* Although Suzanne may have used a broad array of indirect influence techniques, the Confusing technique was the most noticeable and frequent. She did it very well. Many board members, because this voluntary, as opposed to paid activity, was a secondary focus for them, became more and more distant from the operations and returned to the comfort of their former noninvolvement. Was this best for the organization? Who knows? Certainly it was best for Suzanne, but it wasn't necessarily better or worse for board members.

Forgetting or Remembering, Confusing Rather Than Confused

- Confusing can be used effectively to indirectly influence people to be more involved.
- Confusing can also be used effectively to indirectly influence people to be less involved.
- Confusing can be used with individuals and groups and doesn't require an in-depth reading of the individual or group.
- A leader who uses Confusing has to be smart, capable, knowledgeable, credible, and purposeful. Otherwise, he will fall flat on his face, and the target group will think he's an idiot.

Chapter 10

The Columbo Approach

À la Peter Falk

The Columbo approach could also be called the "Confused" approach, but to avoid the perplexity of differentiating the Confused approach from the Confusing approach, I call it the Columbo approach, a term originated by Dr. Donald Meichenbaum.[1] Do you remember Peter Falk, the slightly befuddled, rumpled and disheveled, but always successful, Detective Columbo of TV fame? If you don't, you're definitely younger than I am—and Falk was before your time. He was a memorable character. Columbo always wore a ratty-looking trench coat from which he would reclaim pens, pencils, notes, sunglasses, and other odds and ends from inside or outside pockets, often dropping and misplacing them in the process. He appeared to be extremely disorganized and even somewhat dumb or inexperienced. Still, he always figured out the case and caught the murderer. As a first-time viewer, you were amazed at his successful outcome because Falk seemed so inept. As you continued watching, you came to know what was going on and were amused by the bumbling style that Columbo would use to ultimately and always trap the bad guy.

Part of the fun of watching Columbo's victories was that he went about detecting in such an uncool, apparently ingenuous fashion that his sophisticated suspects were continually disarmed. They were psyched out, faked into thinking he wasn't a threat, not a force to be reckoned with. They generally treated him somewhat disdainfully, or at best as a gnat to be swatted away with mild irritation.

Columbo was a superb indirect influencer, although TV viewers probably never thought of that skill as his claim to fame. But Donald Meichenbaum, Ph.D., a well-known Canadian psychologist and therapist, recognized the utility of the Columbo approach in situations where clients say something that the therapist finds hard to believe, but at the same time recognizes is the client's reality at the moment. "I have absolutely no idea why my husband is unhappy with our marriage. I think we have a beautiful relationship and everything has always run very smoothly between us. I can't imagine why he would just walk out on me with not a hint, a note, or even a good-bye."

As a therapist, a change agent in many ways similar to a manager, you know that a direct approach, in this situation, will not succeed at altering this client's perception. If you say, "I don't believe you. If you don't have a clue that there was a problem and he was perturbed enough to leave, then you certainly cannot have had a beautiful relationship where things always ran smoothly. At best, you must have had bad communication." This kind of comment would put you right in the middle of the client's obvious intrapersonal conflict, escalate the client's denial of a problem, and increase the chance of conflict between the two of you. You may be absolutely correct, but showing her that she's wrong and you're right will put her on the defensive. Competing with her about what she thinks she knows more about than you would come off as offensive. Plus, you are challenging her powerful rationalization about the relationship. This woman needs to hang on to the belief that the relationship was beautiful and there's no explanation for her husband's departure—until she's ready and able to look at some other, perhaps painful possibilities.

Using the Columbo approach, in response to the client's comment that she had no idea why her husband left, you might comment: "That is really strange. Hmm. (Staring into space, pausing, and scratching your head.) I can't understand it myself. Do you have any idea at all, any wild guess, about how he could see things so completely differently from the way you do? (Long, head-shaking pause.) It's hard to imagine." Your goal is for the client then to help you to understand, in your poor confused state.

Nonetheless, you proceed slowly and carefully and never jump in with an "aha" in response to a "wild guess" on the part of the client. You continue to stay somewhat confused. For example, the client says, "He's always been a loyal, steadfast husband. I guess they say the wife is the last to know and if I were to really stretch my imagination, I suppose there could be another woman, but I would seriously doubt it. It just isn't like him and never has been." The therapist wouldn't confirm the client's stretch by saying something like, "In my experience, that's the main cause of men leaving marriages, and I think you're right." Instead, continuing the Columbo approach, the therapist might say, "Hmm, well, as you say, that could be, but it really doesn't make much sense. I don't know. (Staring into space.) This is hard to figure." This kind of approach provides a much safer and slower way for the listener to change than forcing her to acknowledge the serious problems in her marriage that you as the therapist could point out quickly if you used a direct style.

With the use of indirect influence, the therapist is likely to get more information from the client's perspective that will be useful in helping her to adjust than by playing trial and error about the "real" problems in the marriage. Rather than pushing her to accept your expert interpretation of events, you slowly let her, the true expert about her relationship with her husband, explain and elaborate on the marriage to a confused you. Meanwhile, as she attempts to explain to you, she herself comes to formulate some hypotheses about what did happen, and why, and how—hypotheses that help her to understand and to accept the fact that her husband did leave and that there probably was a reason.

In a workshop called "Meaning Reconstruction," psychologist Dr. Robert Neimeyer noted that when he is first interviewing someone he wants to be as "stupid" as he can—to introduce as little in the way of conceptualizations and assumptions as possible in order to let the other person reveal information to him, rather than vice-versa. He suggests that the interviewer be naive and use a "high following" rather than a "high leading" style—following the interviewee's cues, style, words, and belief system, rather than leading with your own cues, style, words, and belief system.

For example, a client says, "I can't believe they really fired me. I've never been unemployed in my life. I still wake up at five every morning and jump in the shower. Then I suddenly remember I don't have a job. But I really forget every night when I sleep." A following style response by you would be to say, "It's a new realization every morning." A leading style response would be "Denial is always a factor in any kind of experience of loss."

Neimeyer says, "Language is the delicate attunement of influence. Be naive. Become a connoisseur of the other person's experience." He talks about the indirect influence approach slightly differently from Meichenbaum, but the principle is the same. Let the client or the other person in the interaction be the expert and tell you his story, rather than becoming the expert and telling him your opinion about his story. You stay confused and help him clarify for you rather than have him be perplexed as you explain for him. [2]

Columbo and Business

Do these examples mean you as a manager have to turn into a therapist to work with your people? No, they don't. But what they do suggest is that you as a change agent, as an influencer of people, one to one, in groups, and in entire organizations, need to have almost an equal breadth and depth of communication skills at your disposal as do therapists in the managed care area. It's no longer adequate for therapists to be purely psychoanalytical in their approach, just as it's no longer adequate for managers to be primarily command-and-control in their approach. And for the same reasons. It doesn't work. It's not cost effective.

For leaders or managers, similar situations can show up in a not-much different costume. One of your direct reports says to you, "I know I guaranteed you that our cash flow problem would be solved by third quarter, but it's still not looking good. Just some system problems that are slowing down the capture of the data. I'm sure by next quarter we'll turn up back where we need to be again. It's just going to take longer than I thought. You know how it goes with any new system."

Your natural response may be to think to yourself, or even to say something like, "Are you kidding me?" or "You can't possibly think I'm going to buy that tired excuse," or "You must think I'm an idiot to give me that bogus story!" Since you know that voicing any version of your thinking would only spur a defensive retort, and, understanding the BA principles, you could instead solicit the person's help in giving you the real poop by using the approach modeled so effectively by Columbo: "Now, wait a minute. I'm a little confused. (Pause, fumble, bumble.) You're telling me that we aren't going to be okay this quarter, but we will be next? That doesn't follow what I thought you thought. I must've misunderstood a lot that's been going on. . . . (Pause, fumble, bumble.)" The good news is that you don't have to wear a ratty-looking old trench coat to pull this off.

The beauty of the Columbo approach is that the other person is thus in the position of having to fully explain the story to you, simply and clearly, because you just don't understand. The goal? To gather more information from the other person's perspective and get the straight facts, rather than defensiveness or excuses on the one hand or unproductive paralysis on the other.

The technique is generally fun and easy to use, more so for managers who already act a little confused naturally than for those who pride themselves on their detail-oriented, superorganized, always-on-top-of-everything approach to work. But it can be a nice change of pace even for those perfectionist types. And it will often be more effective and produce better results than the interrogation approach often favored by those managers who usually know it all.

There are many situations that call for the Columbo approach in management. Let's look first at a standard direct attempt to change the perception of a new hire who reports to you.

Jon: "I'm no better than when I first came to work here. I'm just not catching on as fast as I should. I don't know what my problem is, but I'm really having trouble figuring this job out and getting on top of things."

Manager: "Jon, I know it must be discouraging for you to be having such a difficult time getting into the job, but I do see signs of progress. I'd like you to try to focus more on some of the positive things going on. You have gotten a handle on the software, your reports have definitely improved, and you seem to be fitting in pretty well with the team."

Jon: "But I'm doing nothing compared to how effective I used to be in my old job. I used to have a fast learning curve. Now it's taking me forever to really feel in control of things. I'm not sure if it's poor training, or stress, or just the system here."

This same kind of push-pull could go on forever. Clearly, the direct approach isn't going to work here. What the manager wants in this situation is for the new employee to grab hold, become more confident, get over the transition stage, and take initiative as a strong team member rather than an insecure new employee.

Let's look at what the indirect influence technique, the Columbo approach, would sound like.

Jon: "I'm no better than when I first came to work here. I'm just not catching on as fast as I should. I don't know what my problem is, but I'm really having trouble figuring this job out and getting on top of things."

Manager (*with a genuine look of surprise and confusion*): "You're not any better? Gee, that surprises me. I must have missed some information along the way here (*pause, shuffle through notes, drop pen, put on glasses*) because I thought—well, never mind, I guess I didn't notice that you were going downhill, so to speak. Can you tell me a little more about all the failures you think you're having, because I seem to have missed them?" (*There's some Reframing going on here, as well as Confusion.*)

155

Jon: "Well, it's not that everything is a failure, but I'm just not doing as well as I'd hoped, as quickly as I'd hoped for."

Manager: "So you just aren't making any progress as you see it?" (*Still confused and questioning.*)

Jon: "Well, it's not that I'm not making any progress, but I would like to be making more progress, faster."

Manager: "Do you have any ideas? I really don't know what to suggest. How could you speed up your progress, if that's even possible?"

As the manager, you've already put yourself in the confused, or apparent one-down position, so now putting the monkey of accountability on Jon's back fits. When he makes some of the decisions about how he moves from here to there, he will be more likely to adhere and accomplish.

Research in social psychology, reported in *The American Psychologist*, has demonstrated that "If people can be encouraged to behave in ways that are inconsistent with their attitudes, those conflicting attitudes are likely to change." For example, when experimental subjects role-play in front of an audience by arguing in favor of a given position, they persuade themselves as a result. If Jon, in the example, begins to see himself as accountable for speeding up his progress, inconsistent with his attitude that he's not making progress, he can be persuaded that he is a competent, capable employee. And he can begin to act like he is. [3]

Rita Roberts, a manager who was introduced in Chapter 7, occasionally uses a modification of the Columbo approach. Although she doesn't act confused when talking to her target person, she does act as if he has the answers that Rita doesn't have. Recently, a statewide conference, spearheaded by a consulting group, did not go particularly well. Rather than taking the consulting vendor to task and being critical of his failures, she set up a meeting and asked him to be prepared to discuss with her, and several other staff members:

- What went well
- What went poorly
- Lessons learned

Rita's goal was not to place blame, but to be sure that the consulting company was accountable for what had taken place, acknowledged their responsibility, and realized the changes that needed to take place. She believed that more learning would take place than had she pointed out the error of their ways. The consulting company was put in the limelight as the expert, giving her the answers, rather than her being the expert, telling them what they did wrong. The BA approach worked well and certainly was to the consultant's advantage. Because the consulting company responded well and forthrightly, the relationship was preserved. Nobody became aggressive or defensive, hostile or resistant, angry or counterattacking.

The nonverbal aspects of the Columbo approach are almost as important as what you say to influence others. An approach to handling difficult trainees demonstrates a further refinement of the Confused approach in a nonverbal way. When the disruptive person interrupts or challenges the speaker for the *n*th time, the speaker looks directly at the person, slowly shaking her head back and forth and looking slightly befuddled. The bewilderment is not conveyed as anger or hostility, but more like amazement, as well as Confusion. It is as if you are thinking, "Are you really saying these weird things in this bizarre way?"

Richard Ensman, Jr., talks about nonverbal techniques that you can use particularly when dealing with someone who has an opposing view. He recommends "The Inquisitive Gaze," which he describes as an impassive, slightly puzzled look, and a tilt of the head that conveys mild doubt—"That doesn't sound quite right," your body language is shouting.

157

Ensman says that when you demonstrate this lack of under-standing of the speaker's ideas, nonverbally, you not only cause the speaker to say more, but you subtly force other lis-teners to question the speaker's ideas as well. [4]

The Case

The most common kind of management situation that calls for the Columbo technique is one in which the boss isn't get-ting what he or she feels is the straight scoop from an em-ployee. Here's what an interaction might look like when a manager handles the situation directly, instead of indirectly.

Doreen: "It just seems like we're spinning our wheels here on this project, Roberto. We're going around in circles. First you tell me that the marketing aspect is most important and we need to put our money, time, and energy into materi-als, mailing, and follow-up calls. I buy in and we both put energy into that. Then you say that we really have to perfect the product before we spend more time on marketing. Then you don't answer my questions about your product concerns, but start checking out some ideas with outside consultants. I'm frustrated and discouraged. We've been working on this for three months and we're actually nowhere!"

Roberto: "Well, I'm really back on target now. I don't know what to say. I guess I was a little fragmented there for a while, but I've got the direction now."

Doreen: "How can I believe you? You told me the same thing a month ago. I'll tell you what really blew my mind— when you announced yesterday that the outside consultant would only charge fourteen thousand dollars to reengineer the product and I didn't even know you thought we had product problems. Besides, that's not your job. It's my job to worry about the product. Your job is to take it to market. Yes, we do have to work together, but you seem to have forgotten who does what here."

Roberto: "I think now that our roles are clarified we won't have any more problems."

Doreen: "But I'm the one who just explained that to you. You haven't explained to me anything that makes sense about how this whole thing started out great and has ended up nowhere."

Roberto: "Well, I just don't know what else to say. I understand what you're saying. I agree with you and I'm telling you I'm back on track. What more do you want?"

Doreen: "I'll tell you what I want. I want to know why you even checked with that outside consultant about the product. That makes absolutely no sense to me at all. I can't figure it out. Why would you do that? We don't have the bucks in the first place, but in the second place, that's my job. What were you thinking?"

Roberto: "Well, I guess I was aiming at too much perfection in the product before we took it to market. I thought you'd be glad to get some help on it and we could probably talk the consultant down on the price."

At the end of the conversation, Doreen is more frustrated than at the beginning, and has no more information or understanding about how or why Roberto made his decisions, or why nothing has happened in three months. The more she criticizes him, the vaguer he gets. The more information she throws at him, the less information he returns.

Let's use "The Drill" here to determine retroactively what indirect influence technique would work best. We already know that directness won't work.

The Drill

■ *Decide what you want as an outcome of the communication.* Perhaps Doreen hadn't figured out her specific goal before the conversation and was pressing for information, facts, and the answers so she could understand what went wrong. A clearer goal would be for her to understand what had not worked and then to make a plan with Roberto that would work.

■ *Read the other person in the current situation.* Doreen has known Roberto for a year or so and understands him fairly well. She generally knows what he wants and needs from her—acceptance, approval, and support. She has tried to give him what he wants, but as she looks back, she recognizes that with the current project, for the first time since he began working for her, she has been out of town frequently and consequently less available and less supportive than usual. She also is aware that she had assumed that by now, a year after he had started the job, he could handle this somewhat complex project more independently than previously.

As Doreen thinks about the problem, she recognizes that there is not a good fit operating. There's a mismatch. Whether Roberto is fully aware of the situation at this point or not, he can't get Doreen's approval because there's nothing he can tell her that will make her think something has happened when in fact it hasn't. She won't give approval for no progress, no information, and no plan. What she originally wanted from Roberto was advancement of the project. What she now wants is information about what went wrong, why, and what will be done now to move the project forward.

When Doreen looks back, she also recognizes that Roberto is generally nonassertive with her. He never disagrees or questions her thinking. He is usually compliant and does what she says, without asking questions. But she also remembers that he usually doesn't speak up in meetings and rarely seems to take initiative or introduce new ideas, thoughts, or plans about how to proceed. He looks to her for an okay or a suggestion on most matters.

Doreen definitely has the power in this situation, by the legitimacy of her role as well as by Roberto's apparent need for her approval. In this power differential, however, lies the problem. He is clearly intimidated by her power and her approach, which will result in his being even more nonassertive than usual.

■ *Select an influencing method and technique—direct or indirect.* Doreen had chosen, without thinking, a direct, even occasionally aggressive, approach to Roberto. It didn't work to get her what she wanted and needed from him. This is a good example of a poor choice of the directness decision, because of the disparate needs of Roberto and Doreen, the power differential, and Roberto's general nonassertiveness. Indirect influence would be most likely to result in the outcome Doreen wants.

The Columbo approach seems a perfect fit because it immediately decreases Doreen's intimidation quotient, puts Roberto in a slightly one-up position and her in a slightly one-down position because she's confused and he's not, and encourages a match or fit between their needs.

■ *Implement the technique.* Here's what the beginnings of the conversation might sound like, using Columbo:

Doreen (*Stops by Roberto's desk with several sheets of paper, files, etc., in her arms. Seems harried, but in general, not hostile toward Roberto*): "Roberto, let's get together this afternoon and talk about the McMahon project. I've been gone so much since we started on it that I'm not sure what's going on. I haven't spent any time with you or anyone on it so I feel really out of it. (*Shuffling papers and appearing somewhat disorganized.*) I can't even find my notes from three months ago. (*Appears frustrated but gives up looking and sits down, leaving Roberto standing.*) I give up. Oh, well. Anyway, if you could possibly come by after three P.M. and catch me up about where we are and what we need to do next, I'd really appreciate it. I'm just not on top of things these days.''

This opening leaves Roberto no choice but to agree. Doreen gives him time to put together some sort of presentation and future plan, makes it clear that she's unavailable until they meet, and provides him with appreciation for doing just that. Roberto may soon realize that he won't get the approval that he wants when Doreen finds out what hasn't happened. But he will get recognized for pulling the data together, organizing it, synthesizing it, and planning ahead with it. Doreen will also get what she wants—the information about what has been going wrong with the project, and a Roberto-initiated plan. Her new approach won't resurrect the wasted three months, but neither did her direct approach. And her new approach will leave Roberto in much better shape to get going. At a later date, Doreen can decide how to manage Roberto differently so this kind of problem won't happen again. And perhaps she'll choose to discuss the change with him directly because it will be a different circumstance, a different Doreen, and a different Roberto.

Points to Be Confused About

- The Columbo approach, or the Confused technique, may be difficult for perfectionistic, organized people to add to their repertoire, but it's even more important and useful for them than for more hang-loose managers.
- Reading your target person and determining what he or she wants and needs is critical for effective use of indirect influence. Keep working on it.
- Even if it's unusual for you, a bit of untidiness in appearance, dropping papers, a messy desk, and some

hesitant speech, including a few pauses, uhs and ahs, plus vacant stares can help pull off the illusion. But it's not necessary to do them all at once.

■ The Columbo approach is best used one-to-one, but works as well with aggressive, bully types as it does with nonassertive people. Arrogant listeners get to feeling so superior when you act confused that they often blurt out more than they may have wanted to disclose.

Notes

1. D. Meichenbaum, telephone interview, October 8, 1997. See also D. Meichenbaum and D. Turk, *Facilitating Treatment Adherence* (New York: Plenum Press, 1987).
2. R. Neimeyer, "Meaning Reconstruction and the Experience of Loss," workshop presented Mar. 19, 1999, Mesa, Az.
3. See Basic Behavioral Science Task Force of the National Advisory Mental Health Council, "Social Influence and Social Cognition," *The American Psychologist*, May 1996, pp. 478–484.
4. See R. Ensman, "Discussion, Debate, and Argument: Getting the Upper Hand," *The Toastmaster*, May 1997, pp. 4–15.

Chapter 11

Storytelling and Metaphor

Once Upon a Time

Storytelling is one of the oldest and best-known methods of influencing people, although it is perhaps currently viewed more as entertainment than social influence. Reynolds Price, author of an essay on the origins of narrative, says that telling and hearing stories is more than entertainment or influence. It is "second in necessity apparently after nourishment and before love and shelter. Millions survive without love or home, almost none in silence; the opposite of silence leads quickly to narrative. . . ."

Price discusses prehistoric pictorial narrative, the clear conveyance of stories on cave walls, dating back as far as 32,000 years ago. He also cites biblical tales as evidence of the powerful needs met by storytelling and the early origins of storytelling. He lists the numerous forms of nurturing that storytelling provides, including "the chance that in the very attempt at narrative transaction something new will surface or be revealed, some sudden floater from the dark unconscious, some message from a god which can only arrive or be told as a tale."[1] Perhaps this is a bit of a stretch, but to me Price's comment is a poetic way of describing storytelling as indirect influence.

Stories as Therapy

In the field of psychotherapy, the master storyteller of all time was Milton Erickson, the innovative and creative psychiatrist mentioned previously, who relied almost exclusively on indirect methods of influence to teach and inspire his patients to change.

Erickson often told stories to his patients while they were in a light trance state, a state he thought aided in their openness to change and their acquisition of the learning that would take place. I'm not suggesting here that managers should induce a trace state in employees prior to telling a story to make them more open to the message. But, in many ways, we all somewhat naturally go into a slightly altered state of consciousness when we are listening to a story, as we might when we're watching a TV or movie story. "Once upon a time . . ." can put many of us into a light trance state as we momentarily regress to childhood and the slightly sleepy, soft, soothing, rhythm of bedtime stories.

Michael Liebman, former Clinical Director of the Center for Hypnosis and Psychotherapy at the Milton H. Erickson Foundation taught clinicians how to use stories and metaphor in their work with clients. Now in private practice, he consistently uses stories to accomplish a variety of different outcomes with his clients. Here's a story, in a shortened version, which he recently told to a client, who is a hiker, as is Liebman.

"Recently, I ran into a young woman who was telling me about her experience hiking around Sycamore Canyon. Actually, she reminded me a little of you. She was familiar with the canyon and had hiked a variety of trails there over the last year. This particular day she was alone. She had decided to get away by herself outdoors and just hike randomly, without any clear destination or goal. She wanted to think through a variety of problems that were concerning her.

"She started out on a new trail that started downhill gradually, requiring little concentration. But, then it became strenuous, turning uphill, and demanded more exertion and attention. Part of her wanted to turn back because this wasn't what she had anticipated or wanted. The path continued to get steeper, as did her resistance to putting forth so much energy, particularly as she recognized that she was going further and further into a box canyon. She felt like giving in to her discomfort and kept vacillating between going back and going forward. She told herself to stay with it, but realized that there was no compelling reason to keep on the upward path. But somehow or other she was feeling drawn to continue.

"She was pressing herself and breathing hard when she saw a shaft of light coming through above her, apparently from nowhere. As she came closer, she saw an opening. She couldn't turn back. As she came closer and pulled herself up she saw that the opening was small and narrow, went in deep, and appeared to come out onto the other side. She was tense. She hadn't planned on anything risky, but she thought going through the apparent tunnel was something that she needed to do. And she did.

"There was a wide-open canyon on the other side with a narrow stream, loud frogs, and lush deep grass at the bottom. She hiked down and laid down by the stream, just staring into space, mindless. She didn't know if she slept or not, but when her mind connected back with the moment, she felt comfortable, energized, and relaxed."

No more was said to the client about the hiker or the outcome. What do you guess might be the point of Liebman's story? Would there be any learning that you as a reader could take away? For each individual there may be some unique learning, but many of us could relate to some of these points:

- We often begin an experience with one set of expectations and end up with another, not necessarily better or worse, just different. And that can often be all right.
- Risk-taking can sometimes be more rewarding than caution.
- Although solving problems can be time-consuming, sometimes distraction can speed up the process in unusual ways.
- Learning can take place almost unconsciously.
- Energy expended one way may end up as energy saved in another way.

At some level, in our own mind, we make connections between a story and our life and experiences, as far removed as those experiences might appear to be from the story. Different people will connect in entirely different ways and come up with dissimilar applications to their existence because of their diverse backgrounds.

In telling this story to a new client, Liebman hoped to inspire her with confidence that she would be able to solve the myriad of problems she had brought to therapy. With no further discussion of the story or its application to the client's many problems, she arrived for therapy the next week having concluded that she would let go of a major concern—her parent's lack of willingness to accept her chosen way of life. She realized it just wouldn't happen. She said she saw the decision as a sign of strength on her part, not of giving in or giving up.

Stay in Indirect Mode with Stories

Here's a story that illustrates the way a story can be influential, and also how a storyteller can diminish the impact by mixing direct influence with the indirectness of the story. David Frome, a Phoenix accountant, gave a wonderful speech about two backpacking trips, one with his father and one with his son. The trips were unique in many ways, but to David, the parallelism of his father being thirty-five years older than he, and his son thirty-five years younger, was riveting. It placed him exactly in the middle, chronologically and psychologically. David told us about the spectacular scenery, the glorious weather, and the fascinating hike. Then he talked about the fact that on the trip, his father had seemed almost obsessed with being on time, from the beginning to the end. He kept thinking and speaking in a very linear way: "We have to get up at five A.M. so we can be ready by six so we can be back to the top of the canyon by three and drive home by six P.M." David questioned, "Why? There is no rush." He begged his father not to worry so about time, to enjoy the sights, the sounds, the smells, the quiet and solitude. But his father persisted.

On the other trip, backpacking with his son Derek, David realized in retrospect that he had changed places with his father. He was constantly trying to rush Derek, who wanted to watch and catch lizards, to smell the flowers and peel the bark of trees, to chase a horned toad. "We don't have time now to catch lizards," David scolded his son. "We need to start dinner. Besides, what will we do with it if we catch it? We don't have anything to keep it in and it'll just get away anyway. It's a waste of time." David was suddenly struck by the contrast in his own response to the differences in the time perspective of his father and his son. With both, he was in opposition. David tried to influence his father to slow down, to take time and not rush, to be fully involved with the moment in time. With his son, David tried to influence him to speed up, to think ahead, to give up time on one activity and make it available for another.

David told this story informally, slowly and easily, as if he were just sharing his thoughts and memories with his audience, unrehearsed. It was captivating. We were engaged. We were in an altered state of consciousness. We were all at some time and place in our own lives where we had the same awareness, or where we thought we might apply David's awareness in the near future.

Then David suddenly changed gears. He moved from the storytelling mode to the teaching mode. He moved from indirect influence to direct influence. He called upon us to take action. "So you all need to take some time to think about who in your life you need to take more time with or give more time to. Write it down. Make it a goal. Do it. Time is a gift." On and on he went with his message. *Blah.* The spell was broken. And that's precisely why his evaluator criticized David's otherwise excellent speech. "You had us in the palm of your hand. The subtlety was beautiful. We were all exactly where you wanted us to be. And then you spoiled it all by telling us the moral of the story. And further, you insulted us by acting as if we didn't get it and you had to explain it to us." The evaluator provided a great lesson in good storytelling technique.

Beginning Business Stories

One of the earliest uses of storytelling in business writing, as an indirect influence attempt, came via the book *The One Minute Manager*. The authors, Ken Blanchard and Spencer Johnson, begin the story like this: "Once there was a bright young man who was looking for an effective manager. He wanted to work for one. He wanted to become one. His search had taken him over many years to the far corners of the world. He had been in small towns and in the capitals of powerful nations."

At the time of its publication, 1982, this was an offbeat way for a business book to begin. Inside the front cover, the publisher says: "Read a story that will change your life. *The One Minute Manager* is an easily read story which quickly shows you three very practical management techniques. As the story unfolds, you will discover . . ."

In 106 small pages, with lots of white space similar to children's books, the authors elaborated on one-minute goals, one-minute praisings, and one-minute reprimands. Back then, *The New York Times* called it "One of the more unusual books on the bestseller list!" Since 1982, many similar books have emerged and risen to popularity. How much more fun and less daunting to read a short story than a dry, business-lingo-filled exposition of the same principles.[2]

Leaders and Stories

In the world of business, stories are being touted by respected resources from Tom Peters to *Training and Development* magazine. Not only is the indirect influence technique being suggested as useful, but it is put forth as an essential skill for leaders. Peters says about David Armstrong's book *Managing by Storying Around*, "This book is timeless, because storytelling's power is timeless. But it's timely, too. The marketplace is demanding that we burn the policy manuals and knock off the incessant memo writing; there's just no time. It also demands we empower everyone to constantly take initiative. And it turns out that stories are a—if not *the*—leadership answer to both issues."[3]

In an article on storytelling, "True Tales and Tall Tales: The Power of Organizational Storytelling," the authors, Kaye and Jacobson, point out that stories help us understand in ways that are meaningful and relevant because they are vivid and memorable. They add: ". . . but only recently are stories being recognized as an especially effective means of communication for leaders."[4]

In his book *Leading Minds,* Howard Gardner writes: "The true impact of a leader depends on the story that he or she relates or embodies, and the reception to that story by the organizational audience." Gardner distinguishes between "innovative leaders," who use stories to revive neglected or existing themes that need to be communicated, and "visionary leaders," who create new stories to inspire transformation. They use stories to convince others of a particular view, to create shared meaning and purpose, to help create a sense of community. Gardner continues, "There are a lot of good reasons for the rising interest in storytelling: Many have to do with the power of a story to propel informed change. If experience is a great teacher, then stories based on experience—the storyteller's or others'—may be the next best thing to actual experience. Stories tap into our emotions and intellect in ways that get us to remember and to use the information and wisdom of the past to help us make informed choices in the future."[5]

The leaders in leadership, James Kouzes and Barry Pozner, emphasize storytelling in their 1999 book, *Encouraging the Heart: A Leader's Guide to Rewarding and Recognizing Others.* They discuss the seven essentials of encouraging, one of which is "Tell the Story." They suggest that leaders "Communicate good examples by turning them into good stories."[6]

Dan Stuber, CEO of AETEC, an electronics manufacturing company, is a bright, funny, well-liked leader. He uses Humor, Storytelling, Metaphor, and a variety of other indirect influence techniques in his role as an international business leader. In an interview with me, Dan said that he learned early on in his career that position power was not an adequate resource of power—that personal power was essential. Dan

171

believes that the best way to get people to do what you want them to do is by using a very respectful way of talking to your employees so they themselves will come to the same conclusion that you have arrived at. When you have intelligent employees whom you talk to logically and respectfully as peers, they often absorb and reflect your perspective as their leader, without any direct attempt at influence.

Dan's staff is more likely to see him as funny and as a storyteller than he sees himself, although he recognizes his belief that talking about fun things and making people laugh always equalizes relationships and makes people more comfortable. He does recognize his preference for indirect influence and finds himself more comfortable as well as more effective in the Beyond Assertiveness mode. He is opening a manufacturing plant in Central America as well as one in the United States, and it turns out that this skill is an even stronger asset in Costa Rica because of Costa Ricans' cultural preference for indirectness.

Dan was able to come up with several stories that he uses in different workplace situations. One is a sad, but very versatile and true story. Dan's brother, Steve, had died in an accident about a year earlier. For a variety of reasons, this brother had been the focus of family concern. Could he hold a job? Would he stay out of trouble? Could he afford to retire when the time comes? Would he ever marry again? Could he take adequate care of his son? Suddenly and unexpectedly, Steve died. No one in the family had ever thought about or made a plan for taking care of Steve's son in the event that Steve wasn't able to manage things, much less if he were no longer alive. Dan realized that they had all been worrying about the wrong stuff!

Dan tells this story at work particularly when hard-headed, intelligent, persistent employees are duking it out, verbally, over a certain idea or plan. Although they may have strong feelings about the superiority of their own idea, Dan recognizes that people also have concerns about winning and losing, image, the opinion of others, and how their handling of the issue might affect the way they are approached, seen, or treated in the future. These compelling distractions can get in the way of worrying about the right stuff—what's the best solution to the problem? On several occasions, when he's observed such competitive, interpersonal dynamics taking place in his company, Dan has told the story about his brother and expressed his realization that all of us are often worrying about the wrong stuff. He doesn't give much more detail or direction, but his story alters the opponents' perceptions, and they usually move on to an amicable conclusion and solution.

Metaphors

Scott Sindelar, a professional speaker and psychologist, tells a story using a metaphor. He says, "As speakers, we prepare a speech as a chef prepares a meal. The ingredients attract our patrons. Some guests come invited; some slip in unannounced. We must feed them nourishing stories or they will leave hungry and unsatisfied. Stories that work often have two spicy ingredients. The first is plot. Without it, the story is bland. The story is just a narration of events and actions. Too much plot, however, overwhelms the listeners. They will lose their appetites. They will not hear. A balanced plot creates increasing tension. Tension is the spice of stories. Listeners will stay at the table.

"The second ingredient is deep value structure. The main character is searching for meaning. Using the right spices takes courage and practice. As you create your stories, blend your ingredients into a soaring, compelling tale that will satisfy your listeners. Fill them up and they will leave with enough to share with others."[7]

A story may be a series of metaphors, or one big meta-

173

phor, in and of itself. But of course, a metaphor can stand by itself, not needing a story to surround it. A metaphor is a statement about one thing that resembles something else. It is a statement that contains an implied comparison, for example, the book titles *Riding the Waves of Culture* and *Men Are from Mars, Women Are from Venus.*

In an article entitled "Spice It Up with Figures of Speech," Hartley Engel cites a well-known metaphor. Winston Churchill's use of the phrase "iron curtain," in a 1946 speech, became a staple part of the English language for years. "Beware . . . time may be short . . . from Stettin in the Baltic to Trieste in the Adriatic, an iron curtain has descended across the continent." By using the iron curtain metaphor, which soon became the Iron Curtain, he conveyed clearly and succinctly that the Soviet Union was changing the world as it had been. Not only does this type of powerful metaphor influence people, but it also adds to the impact of the speech. It makes the content more memorable, the message more compelling.[8]

Suzette Elgin, a master writer on the topic of communication, says that everyone is functioning within some metaphor and we all need to learn to identify what other people's metaphors are. We can influence others by matching their metaphors, which are, for them, their realities. In the mainstream American culture, a number of metaphors will turn up over and over again. For example, Elgin cites "The Proud Sailing Ship," a metaphor that encompasses many norms and beliefs:

- Captains go down with the ship.
- Women and children are saved first.
- There's always land ahead.
- For every ship, there's a safe harbor.
- The wind fills our sails because we sail for God and country.
- It's always darkest before the dawn.

- Proud ships always have trusty crews.

- The captain's word is law.

- Proud ships are always tidy and shining, no matter what.[9]

Using and building on the metaphors that seem to guide other people actually combines the techniques of Acting in Accord with Metaphor. Look for signals from others of their metaphors and then use those in return. "We felt driven to do it." "I was flooded with emotion." "I'm carrying too much of the burden of responsibility." Then use the same metaphor to gather more information. For example, "What was the drive like?" or "Has the flood receded yet?" or, "How heavy is the load?" You can also use the metaphor to give advice or a directive. "When the flood recedes you might find unexpected thoughts and plans already planted and growing." Or, "After you've decided to reduce the load you're carrying, you might feel freer to decide where you want to go with your lightened burden." These are all good ways to begin an influence process, by speaking the same language as your audience, whether it is an audience of one or of many.

One of the most dramatic changes I ever produced as a therapist was based on Metaphor. I had a client who had many different day-to-day problems which seemed to stem primarily from his overwhelming, but undeserved, guilt about the suicide of his mother years ago. We had worked together for almost a year with little in the way of apparent change. I had tried all kinds of approaches: support and reassurance, reason and logic, cognitive restructuring, hypnosis, distraction, and systematic desensitization, all to no avail.

Finally I had a brilliant thought. At this point I had nothing to lose, nor did the client. If my great indirect influence technique didn't work, there was no big loss because nothing else had worked either. I asked the client to stop by one day, not for an appointment, but just for a minute. When he came in, I took him into my office and asked him to turn his back to me and lift his shirt up. I then wrote "Mother" on his back in thick, black, felt-tipped pen. I didn't tell him what I had done, but just scheduled another appointment for the next week.

He left confused, but trusting. When he returned, and we talked, it was clear the metaphor had worked. He smiled and said, "It took me all week, but I finally got my mother off my back." I happened to run into this same client several years later and he commented to me that writing on his back was the most helpful part of therapy for him. The effect had lasted. The client had eliminated many of the problems that had stemmed from his leftover guilt about his mother. Who would have guessed the power of this metaphor?

Dan Stuber, the CEO mentioned earlier in the chapter who tells stories well and effectively, also uses metaphors extraordinarily well to influence people. Dan operates three shifts a day at his high-volume electronics manufacturing company. The manufacturing process must be copied exactly every minute, every hour, every shift, every day. There can be no minute deviation from the set system.

In order to maintain quality and consistency, Dan requires shift supervisors to run through a checklist at the beginning of each shift. As you can imagine, the supervisors often resist running through the checklist. From their viewpoint, if everything was running smoothly two seconds before they came on duty, there's no reason to think the checklist will reveal anything amiss. However, what Dan believes is that the majority of manufacturing problems that arise during a shift inevitably prove to be preventable, if the supervisor had only run through the checklist adequately.

Dan has tried talking to the supervisors himself, several times, using a direct influence approach, to no avail. Finally, out of frustration, he developed a great indirect influence that has worked extremely well. Over time, he has met with each shift supervisor, on a random basis, and toward the end of general conversation about life and work he has invited them to go flying with him. Dan is a pilot and owns his own plane. The supervisors are generally enthusiastic about the offer. Then Dan adds, "There's just one limitation you need to know about. I'm not going to go through the pilot's plane checklist before we take off, so you'll have to decide if you're willing to take that risk with your life." Without waiting for a response he says, "We can talk about it more next time I come back. Give some thought to where you want to go." And he leaves.

Dan does come back to see how things are going, and he does take the supervisors flying if they want to go, and of course he does use the flight checklist when he flies. But he has made his point well with a metaphor and he never makes it more direct. The supervisors get the message loud and clear, and increase the use of their own checklists accordingly.

The Drill

In case you might be influenced by now to become a part-time storyteller, and even use a metaphor or two to influence people, let's discuss how you might do that best. We'll use an adaptation of the six-step system for a guide, but use it to plan a story rather than to look restrospectively at storytelling as an indirect influence technique.

■ *Decide what you want as an outcome of the communication.* It's of ultimate importance to know what message you're trying to send, what influence you're hoping to have, what point you want to make with the story. What are you trying to accomplish by using Storytelling? Are you trying to motivate and encourage your employees? Do you want to inspire them to work harder? Do you want them to hang in during a tough time? Do you want them to increase their loyalty to the company?

Since we're in the planning mode, let's decide that you want to inspire your senior management team to work together more cooperatively and less competitively. You've talked to them directly before, but gave up because it just didn't seem to work. You know your senior staff respects you, but your own history reeks of an aggressive rather than collaborative style. They may not have believed you meant what you said when you told them directly. They may also have generated some resistance to your message. It has been a month since you gave it the last direct shot, with no visible change, although you've consistently modeled more collaborative behavior with them. You've decided to bring in a full range of indirect influence techniques, including Storytelling.

■ *Read the audience—of one, or many.* When you tell a story, it must be directed very accurately at the audience. Just as you would tell a totally different story to a six-year-old than you would to a ten-year-old, you would tell a different story to a group of men than a group of women, to field employees rather than corporate managers, or to people who are for you versus people who are against you. It could be the same basic story, but slightly changed and modified to fit the intended audience.

A priest at the church I sometimes attend told a good story one morning. He described a fairytale village where everyone was happy and life seemed to proceed harmoniously for all. Unfortunately, the happiness was jarringly interrupted by the sudden and unexpected death of the thirteen-year-old son of a middle-aged village couple. The mother was inconsolable. Her friends and family, her faith and inner strength, were not enough to help. Her sadness overwhelmed her. She sought help from ministers and physicians, faith healers, and psychologists, from soothsayers and metaphysicists, but nothing helped. Finally, she came upon a learned guru, living a solitary existence in a small cave, and asked him for advice. He said, "Go to each family in the village until you've found one that has not suffered. Then bring me a cup of milk from that family, and you will be healed!"

The mother of the deceased child was cheered. She knew that in her happy village, she could quickly find someone who had experienced no suffering. But as she went from door to door, she found that no matter how happy and comfortable each family seemed, each had at some time experienced extreme pain, hurt, and suffering. She also found that they had all recovered from their pain. Not that they didn't remember it, but they had moved beyond it. She returned to the guru, without the requisite cup of milk, but with a different mindset. She was healed.

Take a quick moment and figure out how this story, in a different shape or form, could be altered to effectively bring about a change in your colleagues or the people who report to you—without coming across as "preachy"! Customize it to your read of your specific audience. I've included some sample stories later in this chapter.

For the story that you'll be developing to tell the senior management team, you have read them to be somewhat resistant, perhaps in general cynical, smart, and a bit arrogant. They are definitely left-brained people with analytical minds. They are all men, and all sports enthusiasts. You know it will take more than one story to change their thinking and behavior, but what you've tried hasn't worked, so you decide you have nothing to lose by trying something else.

■ *Decide what and how you're going to tell the story. Sell!ng* magazine advocates Storytelling as an indirect influence technique in the article "How to Sell with Sizzle Stories." The author, Art Sobczak, says that "the more interesting you make your sales message, the more impactful and memorable it will be. When your customers can 'see' and 'feel' why they should buy, they often do it.'' Sobczak makes some suggestions:

- Put your potential customer in the story.
- Use word pictures.
- Animate and humanize products and services.
- Share personal experiences.
- Use humor.
- Personalize the story to your audience.

These same suggestions may also fit for managers working to develop a story that will sell an idea, an attitude, or a behavior to their internal customers, their employees.[10]

In the case of the aggressive senior management team, you know that there are some points you definitely want to make:

- Working as an integrated, cooperating team is ''in,'' and will be rewarding as well as rewarded.
- Working as individual competitors is ''out,'' and will be punished.
- Being flexible and adapting quickly to change is a new requirement of the job.

There are all kinds of possibilities for stories. Before I give you a sample, take a minute and see if you can think of a story that you could tell that would fit the bill, that would increase the likelihood that you would achieve the outcome you want. The story can come from your own experience, or from something you heard or read about, or could be a story that is already known to members of your audience, but known from and in a different setting—for example, children's stories, myths, fables, and fairy tales, or even corporate tradition tales. Remember, you're trying to make an important point, but in an indirect way. The story needs to be subtle, not a whack to the side of the head. You're influencing your group indirectly because the direct way didn't work, so make sure you don't interject a moral to the story.

■ *Telling the story.* When you tell a story to this group of senior managers, timing is important. You want to embed the story in an everyday context, rather than pull it out immediately after some "bad" behavior. Then it can appear unintentional, rather than like a lesson imposed by you as punishment. So, for example, you might tell a story that conveys your theme when your team is talking about their weekend, or discussing the basketball playoffs, or talking about a new product that's being developed. But you wouldn't want to tell it right after an acrimonious interchange between several senior mangers at a staff meeting.

Here are a couple of stories that might work for the group mentioned above.

"Anybody watch the playoff game this weekend?" (After some general discussion, you introduce the story, which came from *USA Today*.) "I read an unusual story about Avery Johnson and David Robinson yesterday. Maybe you've heard this before, but I hadn't. These two guys are both very competitive guys but also very close friends. Apparently the similarities they share, in addition to their common cause on the court, are much more powerful than their differences. They both are driven by their desire for the ring. But here's what's really unusual to me. Johnson was quoted as saying he wanted to win a championship more for Robinson than he did for himself—he wanted to see him succeed even more than himself. Then, to top that, Robinson is quoted as saying, 'The great thing about this team is guys care more about each other than they do about themselves.' I don't know. That kind of thinking is a huge shift from the basketball egos we're used to, and almost seems to defy belief, but it sure has worked well for the Spurs."[11] And you say no more.

Then, later that same week, you might mention Phil Jackson and the Lakers. "Things have really changed with Jackson at the helm for the Lakers. I guess he has a way of making everyone on the team want to work together and really want to be on the team. He gets the most out of every individual player, but still manages to get them to play as a team. Amazing! You know what was most interesting to me was that the article in *USA Today* characterized Jackson as being out on the fringe, with one foot planted in reality. I didn't really get that until I saw a description of his philosophy: Everyone's different, you can't expect people to all act alike, and you can't treat them all alike, not if you want to get them to understand each other, accept each other, and sacrifice for each other. The writer called it quirky stuff. Interesting that a philosophy like that, which doesn't seem far out to me, just seems sane, even if a break with the old ways, is viewed as far out. I guess I'd consider it not on the fringe, but on the leading edge."[12] And you say no more.

The story or stories may take a few months to begin to elicit the kind of behavior you're looking for, but as soon as it happens you need to start reinforcing the collaborative behavior, still indirectly; not, "I'm glad you finally got it, Joe, and have decided to be a team player," but just, "Thanks for your contribution, Joe, you really added value to the problem-solving process."

The Tale End

- Once upon a time, we all talked in stories and listened to stories.

- Stories and metaphors are powerful ways to influence

individuals and groups, whether they are receptive or resistant.

- Learning to use this kind of indirect influence is fun, interesting, and mind expanding for the leader as well as the followers.
- And then, everyone can live happily ever after.

Notes

1. See R. Price, *A Palpable God* (New York: Atheneum, 1978).
2. K. Blanchard and S. Johnson, *The One Minute Manager* (New York: Berkley Books, 1982).
3. T. Peters, review of David Armstrong's *Managing by Storying Around*. Amazon.com, July 1999. See also D. Armstrong, *Managing by Storying Around* (New York: Doubleday and Co., 1992).
4. B. Kaye and B. Jacobson, "True Tales and Tall Tales: The Power of Organizational Storytelling," *Training and Development*, March 1999, pp. 44–50.
5. H. Gardner, *Leading Minds* (New York: Basic Books, 1995).
6. J. Kouzes and B. Pozner. *Encouraging the Heart: A Leader's Guide to Rewarding and Recognizing Others* (San Francisco: Jossey-Bass, 1999).
7. S. Sindelar, personal communication. See also S. Sindelar, "President's Minute Message," *The Arizona Speaker*, January 1999, p. 2.
8. H. Engel, "Spice It Up with Figures of Speech," *The Toastmaster*, February 1999, p. 23.
9. S. Elgin, *The Last Word on the Gentle Art of Verbal Self-Defense* (New York: Prentice Hall, 1987).
10. See A. Sobczak, "How to Sell with Sizzle Stories," *Sell!ing*, November 1998, p. 12.
11. The source of this story is G. Boeck, "God, Family and Friends," *USA Today*, June 16, 1999, p. 2C.
12. The source of this story is D. Dupree, "Lakers Can Expect Big Changes," *USA Today*, June 17, 1999, p. 1C.

Chapter 12

Humor

The Most Fun

President Reagan was famous for his frequent on-target humor. As he lay on the operating table after the assassination attempt in 1981, the president reputedly said to the surgeons gathered around his draped and prepared body, "I hope you guys are all Republicans." He illustrated well the indirect influence effect of humor. People who use it, particularly in stressful or seemingly one-down positions, are viewed as being on top of things, being in charge and in control, whether they are in fact or not. Leaders are sometimes reluctant to use humor because they fear it will reduce their credibility, but in fact it usually enhances their perceived status. Audiences will take you seriously more of the time if they see you can afford to abandon seriousness some of the time.

Ellie Marek, humor expert and author of *Eating Roses: Bites of Living Humor*, has a lot to say on the topic of humor and influence and was influential enough to have me include her comments in this chapter.

One of the most powerful and overlooked indirect influence techniques is humor—a.k.a laughter, play, and wit," she writes. "When it comes to using humor as a resource, we often dismiss its significance, or worse, we succumb to the myth that there is no place for humor when the goals are serious. As Woody Allen put it, 'Humor never gets to sit at the grownups' table.' That's a shame, because humor is one of the best safeguards of sanity available to today's leaders. In a world given to enormous excess and frightening extremes, a healthy sense of humor is one way of keeping a balance between gullibility and cynicism.

Humor can be a powerful ally in communication. First, humor eases tension and lightens the atmosphere, in both personal and business relationships. Laughter has the guaranteed result of releasing tension. When a working environment becomes very tense, it is too late to yell, "Lighten up!" A leader has to show and demonstrate the way, every day. The goal is always to influence people to take their work seriously, while they take themselves lightly. When people take themselves too seriously, they become very defensive. When people can laugh together and appreciate a common joke—an "in-joke"—a strong bond is formed, and resistance disappears. Shared humor that doesn't put anyone down allows us to identify with one another, and hopefully to learn to laugh at ourselves. Messages rejected when said directly are accepted when said with humor. Humor is the bit of sugar that makes the medicine go down.

Leaders can create a lighthearted environment with such simple things as gag signs. My favorite office sign hangs just inside the door of a very busy, often harassed, hospital administrator: "All who come through this door bring joy. Some when they enter and some when they leave." Everyone who enters that office is at least optimistic about a pleasant outcome, recognizing that the administrator has a sense of humor. In this kind of relaxed environment, communication advances one step further and people are more receptive to influence.

The jargon of the day is an excellent way to create humor bonds in a work setting. There are certain clichés that are overused ad nauseam, such as "share" and "special." But they are so popular that only with the most "special" colleagues can you "share" your weariness with these words. Just about every family and company or department has its own in-jokes, which when called forth can almost immediately influence all to move on, to get energized.

When I first started working in the early 1970s, we working mothers were sure we could become master jugglers and balance it all, at least if we acquired the prerequisite standard accessory for the seventies working woman. Some smart entrepreneur sold the group of new working women on the idea that the key to a professional image was a wig. Most of us bought carefully coiffed wigs, styled and stiff, with never a hair out of place. They gave us terrific headaches, but that was a small price to pay for the image.

One night I came home with my attaché case, my wig, and my headache, and walked into total chaos. The living room was decorated with discarded shoes, jackets, papers, and books. The only signs of food preparation were a few open cans of Coke and some bags of potato chips. Background music was high-decibel stereo and TV. Every voice was raised. The scene so clashed with my fantasy of peace, harmony, order—and dinner on the table—that for reasons I still do not understand, I literally blew my top. I grabbed my wig and hurled it full force into the center of the room. I was screaming terrible threats. However, within seconds, all of us dissolved into hysterical laughter. Within minutes, calm, quiet, and dinner—quickly prepared by the children—appeared.

It is true that I could never have strategized my reaction as an intentional indirect influence technique, but we did have a family culture that encouraged the use of humor as influence. And since that time, "Don't blow your top, Mom" has become a family code. Family sayings and family jokes are often the very best ways of lifting the weightiness and at the same time making a clear point. In our family, my grandmother used an old Irish saying to put an end to pointless arguments on differences of taste or opinion. " 'Everyone to his own taste,' said the old woman as she kissed the cow."

In the stress-filled workplace of today, humor and play workshops are being offered as ways to keep workers happy and loyal, as are flexible schedules, child care, and in-house workout rooms. In many of these workshops, props such as bamboo finger traps and scarves for juggling double as humor, play, and metaphors. When you put your fingers in each end of the finger trap and pull, you can't get them out no matter how hard you try. You have to relax and let go. Juggling is a pretty obvious metaphor for what we do in our personal and working lives. Juggling scarves looks like fun, but it takes practice and skill. Juggling life doesn't even look like fun and takes even more practice and concentration. Both can bring us zest and color.

People can't hold two opposing emotions simultaneously. If laughter or humor displaces anger or frustration even for a few moments, an opportunity for influence appears. There are many lessons to be taught and bought in the corporate world, and both are done best when laughing.[1]

Many experts, in addition to Marek, have words of wisdom to contribute about the value of humor as a positive influence technique, but some are more cautious. Frons Trompenaars, an expert on culture, notes that humor across cultures rarely works: The language obscures the humor, the jokes rely on "in-country" allusions and knowledge, or the setting and type of humor accepted is narrowly guided by specific country norms.[2] George Simons, a diversity and humor-as-influence proponent, also acknowledges that workplace humor can be a minefield. He suggests some guidelines for avoiding disastrous consequences:

- First-person experience is the best because it's fresh, told about oneself, and the least likely form of humor to be rejected by others.
- Use humor to lighten a situation, not to make light of it. Humor can provide the right dose of lateral thinking that can bring us out of gridlock in a meeting. It can be used to bond and to resolve a challenge.
- Study humor so you'll continue to learn how to use it most effectively.
- Get participation from others—their responses, their ideas, their humor.[3]

Many people think the political correctness stance, and its concern about offending people, has put a crimp in our

American style of humor. From the PC perspective, humor is still seen as an indirect influence technique, but proponents are concerned that too often the result is negative. Receivers don't change their perspective positively or open their minds. Instead, they are offended. Their resistance, opposition, and defensiveness are increased rather than reduced.

Interestingly, at the International Humor Conference I recently attended, there were dramatically different viewpoints about the use of gender and ethnic humor. Opinions ranged from "It's all about the intentions of the teller" to "Ethnic and gender humor is a celebration of difference" to "If the receiver is supersensitive, tough, that's his or her problem" to "There's so much great humor that's not sexist or racist or offensive, why would anyone with good intentions not use it?"

As an indirect influence technique, where you're trying to change someone's perspective, reduce resistance or resentment, or get her to change her behavior, any kind of joke or humor that is at her expense personally, or may even possibly offend her generally, won't work. It has nothing to do with political correctness, but instead with practicality. It will interfere with your getting what you want as an outcome and probably increase the likelihood that the target person won't do what you want her to do.

Men and Women

Men tend to be more comfortable with using humor freely in the workplace than are women. And their humor of choice is put-down humor and jokes. When men are working together, or meeting together, inevitably someone will start the cycle, "Did you hear the one about . . . ?" And then an apparent competition ensues, with each man adding his best or newest joke to the lineup. It seems to be as much a part of the get-together as an agenda. Generally this use of humor doesn't seem to have a specific influence outcome desired, but rather to lighten things up, to build camaraderie and teamwork in a general sense.

This same kind of humor doesn't work well with women. A recent survey that Ellie Marek and I conducted with 114 men and women found that women were much more frequently offended by put-down humor, of men and of women, than men were. Men found the humor—even about themselves—to be funny much more frequently than women did. Obviously, then, male managers should be more judicious about using any kind of put-down humor with women than with men. That's just good adaptive communication.

Women traditionally have used self-deprecating humor with each other, in social and business settings. They put themselves down, instead of each other, as men do. Unfortunately, that kind of humor can detract from the person's credibility, unless she has lots of it and can afford to take the hit. Generally, in the world of business, women are still viewed as having less credibility than men, so they're better off to eliminate the self-put-down. In contrast, using a bit of self-put-down humor can work extremely well for men to influence an audience of women to see them as accessible and on the same wavelength.

Perhaps because women express a concern that they're still not taken seriously in the workplace, they may tend to take themselves too seriously. Actually, they need to use even more humor as leaders than men do, to take advantage of the credibility-building boost they can get, just like Ronald Reagan. They need to use humor that fits for them, such as stories and anecdotes about their own experiences, rather than jokes and put-downs. If they have enough credibility, they can occasionally use a put-down of themselves with women. Unless they are truly intimidating in the aggressiveness of their style, they still shouldn't use that self-deprecatory style with men.

Humor and Therapy

Humor has arrived officially, but belatedly, in the therapist's office. Undoubtedly, therapists have been using it surreptitiously for years, but the great okay from the sky has arrived only recently in the form of an article in the *APA Monitor*, the newspaper of the American Psychological Association. The article, "Therapists See New Sense in Use of Humor," surprisingly showed up on the *Monitor*'s front page. In this staid monthly publication that focuses on the "big issues" in psychology—research, politics, and policy—an article on the utility of humor in therapy was even more unlikely than an article on humor in the funeral directors' monthly newsletter.[4]

Perhaps because suicide and mental illness, divorce and grief, anxiety and depression—the grist of the therapy mill—don't immediately seem like topics to laugh about, humor has been a belated tool among the therapist's influence tactics, along with toys and play, with adults as well as children. Certainly the clients, the carriers of the burdens, don't seem ideal candidates for humor as influence targets. They aren't feeling lighthearted, they often aren't thinking clearly, they're preoccupied and forgetful, extremely self-absorbed and narrow in their thinking due to their problems. They often are not thinking creatively, to say the least. Clients in therapy are often very sensitive and could quickly feel put down or take the humor personally rather than benefiting from it. It can seem like a risky approach for a therapist to take. And it may well be. But in the shrink underworld, there is a quiet revolution going on. Therapists are using humor much more frequently, benefiting their clients, having more fun, and generating creative energy for themselves in the process.

At the International Humor Conference, one session focused on therapeutic humor—humor used to attend or treat disorders through remedial methods. The focus was on the use of humor to change our internal environment, particularly when we can't change our external environment. Although this session was primarily about the use of humor with physical conditions, a nurse, Patti Wooten, told a story about a seriously depressed patient who had stopped herself from jumping off a bridge by recognizing some humor in the situation. As she looked down to get ready to jump, she noticed that she had on a pair of $150 shoes that she had bought in the last week. She heard herself say, to herself, "I don't want to ruin those expensive shoes by getting them all wet." She then realized how silly that comment was, considering that she was thinking of killing herself by jumping into the river, getting her whole self totally wet, and drowning. She laughed at the absurdity. The sudden change in her internal environment, her perspective, made her realize she still had some energy to continue her struggle with life.[5]

The author of the *Monitor* article, Patrick McGuire, suggests that a humorous response that is consciously chosen and used on the part of the therapist produces the greatest likelihood of success. McGuire notes that comedy deals with a shift in perspective and allows people to see something differently, or feel something differently, so the therapist needs to know exactly what shift in perspective he or she is trying to accomplish. When the humorous comment is made without a plan, it may make the client laugh, but may not produce a difference in perspective. That certainly doesn't hurt, but it also may not help. If therapists use humor strategically, on the other hand, they can increase their ability to help people solve problems, alter their priorities, and feel better overall.

McGuire quotes Ed Dunkleblau, Ph.D., who says that the raw material of comedy and therapy are the same: "Both deal with tragedy, suffering and conflict—you don't make jokes about things that are not serious." Dunkleblau suggests a checklist for clinicians interested in using more humor in therapy, which is just as useful for leaders who are interested in using more humor at work:

- Look for organizations of professionals who are serious about humor.
- Surround yourself with funny people.
- Make a deal with yourself to play every day.
- Keep a funny audiotape in your car (and office) for use in emergencies.
- Observe your surroundings for humor—kids, animals, people, and events.
- Clip cartoons and funny quips and quote or post.[6]

I started using humor as a therapist about eighteen years ago, when I also began doing professional speaking. Since graduating from college, I had become a very serious person: wife of a physician, Ph.D. psychologist, mother of four, college professor, and therapist. I took myself, and my work, very, very seriously. Consequently, I was frequently drained of energy and somewhat pessimistic.

As I began to speak to groups about mental illness and therapy, I noticed a certain lack of responsiveness from the audience, even though my talks were full of useful information and basically well crafted. I couldn't figure it out, but I decided to join Toastmasters and get better at speaking.

I learned a great deal through Toastmasters, and I'm still learning, but the first major hit over the head for me was that no matter how serious the topic, I had to inject some humor into my talks or I'd no longer be asked to speak. I realized, too, that I had much more fun, and was consequently more energetic and enthusiastic, when I was speaking with humor rather than without it. I learned another important lesson from the renowned speaker and founding father of the National Speakers Association, Cavett Robert. When asked "Do you always have to use humor in your speeches?" he replied, "Only if you want to get paid." I did.

As I began to use more humor in speaking, I found that I

felt, thought, and acted funnier in general in life, and also as a therapist. I enjoyed being a therapist more, and the lighter approach seemed to have beneficial effects on my clients. More often than not, I was successful in changing the perspective of the client. Occasionally, however, I misjudged a client, resulting in their leaving therapy, at least with me.

The most notable of these misjudgments took place with a young woman who had extremely low self-esteem. Anything and everything negative that happened on her entry-level job, she took the blame for. If the boss was in an irritable mood, it was because he was mad at her for some unnamed error. If an order was delayed, it was because she hadn't completed her part on time. If a customer expressed a complaint, it was because she hadn't answered the phone in the right way. Her self-blame was endless and self-absorbed, as well as without reason. I had tried a variety of approaches to bring about a change in her internal thinking, all to no avail.

I wanted my client to recognize that everything that went on at her job was not related to her, as a way of turning around the stream of self-criticism. I finally concluded that writing a message on the knee of her jeans, which she always wore to work, would be a great and constant reminder. Since she always looked down, she would constantly see the message, and because I would write it for her eyes, others wouldn't really be able to read it, and even if they could, they wouldn't know what it meant. When she was feeling confident enough to start looking up, the message would be unnecessary.

So when the next appointment time came, I was ready and armed with a felt-tipped pen.

My client began her usual litany of self-blame: "It was all my fault." "I messed up again." "I shouldn't have said that." "I didn't do it right." As she continued, I leaned forward and wrote on her left knee "NOT," and on her right knee "ME." Since we had discussed this idea many times, I thought she would find this reminder as funny and playful as I did. Wrong. She not only didn't find it funny, she was offended and annoyed. She also quickly demanded that I pay her, now and in cash, for a new pair of jeans! I did, and she left.

The only solace for my mistake was that the client did, at least with me, stand up firmly for her rights, and she blamed me convincingly for this error, rather than herself. I'll never know if it lasted or not.

Humor and Business

In many management situations, formal or informal teaching and learning are, or should be, taking place. As the authority figure, the manager could undoubtedly increase his or her influence, as well as the positive attitude and retention of learning by the recipient, with humor. Certainly, learning and teaching are part of getting people to do what you want them to do. On-the-job training is often the responsibility of management. Teaching is often an implicit aspect of leadership. And humor is a great way to increase your influence as a teacher. Debra Korobkin, author of an article called "Humor in the Classroom," says, "Humor as a diagnostic and facilitating strategy for teaching and learning is only now being investigated. Students and teachers with a sense of humor are sought after for their ability to set people at ease, equalize situations and status relationships, find unexpected connections and insights, and increase group rapport."[7]

Theoretically, humor also unleashes creative thinking and opens learners to divergent thinking, but the actual empirical research investigating the relationship between humor and adult learning is sparse and ambiguous. There is some basis for the belief that humor in the learning context increases retention of material and productivity and decreases academic stress and anxiety about the subject matter.

Good, adaptive humor is a great way to win over, or at least to not lose, any audience you have reason to believe is not entirely with you. It might not be against you to start with, but it also might not be for you—for example, if you have bad news to deliver to a group, or you're leading some unpopular mandatory training, or things haven't been going well and you're going to have to talk about the consequences.

When you share some laughter about a common experience, you've already connected on the similarity-bias wavelength and you're in a much better position to then lead the other person where you want her to go. You've already led her to humor, you've influenced her to laugh, so she is much more ready and willing to go with you where you want to go.

Scott West, VP of marketing for Van Kampen, was presiding over a question-and-answer session with regional VPs. The idea was to answer any and all questions at the beginning of a long day of presentations about programs and products. The question-and-answer session at the start of the day was in itself a good indirect influence technique. By opening himself, his leadership, his department, and his strategy up to being challenged, criticized, and possibly rebuked by twenty-plus aggressive people, Scott came across as being very much in control of his job, himself, and any potential problems. And there was a plethora of concerns, criticisms, and problems. He let the session go on until he had literally exhausted all comments and questions.

To add to Scott's influence during the session, he used frequent quick, dry humor, which furthered people's perception that he really was on top of things. When asked about some marketing materials that had been delivered with typographical errors, he commented, "Yeah, one keystroke and I screwed the whole thing up. Can you imagine? Just one little keystroke in the middle of the night as I was pecking away at that thing." When the questioner persisted, Scott persisted too. "Guess you didn't hear me. Yeah—I made a mistake! I definitely did. I write all these things myself, you know." Clearly, the problem was one over which he had no control, but rather than blaming other people, other departments, he just joked about it and pretended personal responsibility and blame. But there wasn't a hint of hostility or sarcasm in his delivery.

A later question addressed the need for an in-house speaker to represent the company at certain events. Scott mentioned several people who had been used successfully in the past and explained why they weren't using these people now but were using Sam instead. The follow-up question was, "Well, I haven't heard Sam or seen Sam on the circuit. Has anybody else? Is he good? What's going on with him?" Scott's reply: "Well, I really wanted to get Sam in the limelight. He could be a great spokesman for the company. I've been working on it for the last six months. Unfortunately, I just found out some bad news. Sam doesn't like traveling. He doesn't like doing radio or TV. He doesn't like speaking. And he doesn't want to be in the limelight! That's what's going on with Sam." All of this was said with a slightly confused look, a little self-deprecation, and a smile. Everyone laughed and there were no more questions on the topic.

Finally, one of the participants asked about the Y2K problem. He said he had heard some "weird stuff" about "problems ahead." Scott, in professorial manner, said, "Yes, you can read my white paper on the topic next week. We call it a white paper because that's exactly what it is. A big sheaf of white paper with nothing on it." Again, everyone laughed, and no one asked anything more about Y2K. With his use of humor, Scott had successfully influenced the group to believe that there was no problem at all—or if there was, he had it under control. The success of his influence attempt was demonstrated when the group, a somewhat resistant and unruly bunch to start with, gave him a loud and spontaneous round of applause when he concluded.[8]

Scott demonstrated a point made by Robert Orben in an article in *The Toastmaster*. Orben wrote, "In recent years, humor has gone from being an admirable part of a leader's character, to being a mandatory one. . . . Business executives and political leaders have embraced humor because humor works." Orben reinforces the point made earlier in relation to former president Reagan. "One of the reasons we respond to people with a sense of humor is that humor implies control and command of a situation. . . . Humor is the ultimate expression of being, cool, calm and collected. It . . . influences thinking and attitudes and helps reassert control."[9]

Get Serious about Humor

- Humor is such a powerful indirect influence technique that if you're not using it as a leader, you have a great excuse to spend money and time loosening up and gaining some "laugh ability."
- The more out of control you are, or the situation is, the more important is your ability to pull some laughs out of the hat.
- If you think you're too important or serious or prominent to use humor, you've failed the emotional intelligence test.
- If you're feeling desperate and hopeless as a humorous leader, buy an audio track that is just pure laughter. Listen with a friend and you'll both be on the floor within three minutes.

Notes

1. Taken from a conversation between the author and Ellie Marek.
2. F. Trompenaars, *Riding the Waves of Culture* (London: The Economist Books Ltd., 1993).

3. G. Simons, "The Uses and Abuses of Humor in a Multicultural World," *Managing Diversity* 7:1 (October 1997), pp. 1, 3.

4. P. McGuire, "Therapists See New Sense in Use of Humor," *APA Monitor* 30:3 (March 1999), pp. 1, 10.

5. 1999 ISHS International Humor Conference, Martin Lampert, Chair, Oakland, California, June 29–July 3, 1999.

6. Ibid.

7. D. Korobkin, "Humor in the Classroom: Considerations and Strategies," *College Teaching* 36:4 (Fall 1988), pp. 154–158.

8. S. West, Regional Sales Meeting, June 1999.

9. R. Orben, "Why Humor?", *The Toastmaster*, March 1993, pp. 6–7.

Chapter 13

Success with Subtlety

"You can catch more flies with honey than with vinegar" is the metaphor that Dan Stuber used to deal with a conflict between two senior managers. A plant manager, Carlos, had been hired to set up and run a new manufacturing facility for Dan, in a distant geographic location. Although Dan would be visiting frequently, Carlos was definitely in charge. The buck stopped there. And Carlos was pleased and comfortable with the responsibility and control.

After a few months, it was necessary to hire a second senior-level manager, Francisco, who understood more than Carlos about the business practices, the rules and regulations of the country, the governmental agencies and their department heads to be contacted, in preparation for setting up a manufacturing facility. Carlos's expertise was in the manufacturing process itself.

Within a month of Francisco's arrival, Carlos was clearly unhappy. Although Francisco's role was clearly secondary to that of Carlos, it was essential, and Carlos often found himself in the position of making manufacturing process decisions based on Francisco's recommendations—a circumstance he did not like, but had to accept. Francisco was a very direct, even occasionally aggressive communicator and influencer, while Carlos was normally a more indirect and low-key influencer. He felt steamrolled by Francisco and began to seethe with resentment.

Although previously Carlos had functioned independently, now he called Dan frequently to discuss and complain about the problems with Francisco. Dan did not want to take the control away from Carlos, for many reasons. On the other hand, he did not want Carlos to continue calling him about the problem. After turning the discussion back to Carlos several times and offering several action options without apparent dissipation of Carlos's concerns or calls, Dan tried something different. In a phone call that began as usual with Carlos's expression of frustration, Dan said, "Carlos, I remember that you spent a lot of time as a young adult living in Kansas. And I know you liked it there and enjoyed going to college at the University of Kansas. What I also know is that everyone from Kansas knows something that I'm sure you know, too. You can catch more flies with honey than with vinegar."

There was a long pause in the telephone conversation. Carlos understood. Without further discussion, Carlos took full responsibility for handling the conflict. And although the problem between Francisco and Carlos wasn't completely resolved with the honey solution, the problem between Carlos and Dan was.

One of the most enjoyable aspects of the indirect influence approach is the pleasure that you as a leader can experience as a master of the elegant solution. Anyone can hammer a square peg into a round hole with enough brute force, but it's generally not particularly pleasurable for the wielder of the hammer, the peg, or the round hole. Not everyone can solve a potentially devastating interpersonal or group conflict with as much calmness, indirectness, and finesse as Dan did. And when he was done, no one—not Carlos, not Dan, and not Francisco—felt bruised or abused.

When I think of some leaders who are currently popular and well known, not perhaps for their use of the Beyond Assertiveness approach but for the noticeable absence of a command-and-control approach, the CEO of Southwest Airlines, Herb Kelleher, comes to mind. He's known for his antics, his gimmicks, and his hang-loose philosophy—so much so that a book written about him and his company is called *Nuts!*[1]

I just flew on Southwest and enjoyed the wackiness of the flight attendants—one of whom did an Elvis impersonation as he was giving us those tedious instructions about seat belts and oxygen masks, while the other sang to us as we landed. I know, and you do too, that results like that can't happen as a result of a manager telling a flight attendant, "You will do an Elvis impersonation on takeoff for every flight you're on, and you will write and sing a song for every landing." No, I don't have the inside scoop here. But I can't believe that these two people, a man and a woman, would so enthusiastically, seemingly spontaneously, and laughingly produce such results unless they wanted to do it. And why would they want to do it? Because Kelleher modeled and otherwise indirectly influenced them to be that way and to do those things. The same result could not have been accomplished with a direct influence approach.

As a leader, you can also experience a very enjoyable high by achieving your goal, getting your employees to do what you want without the struggle and the sweat, without their consciously being aware that you're influencing them, and with the more positive feelings from them that come from not feeling coerced, bullied, intimidated, or resentful. It's a pleasantly satisfying feeling, like taking a long, scenic, slow run instead of completing a series of sprints, or eating a light, delicious, unusual meal, rather than a heavy, filling one of steak, mashed potatoes, and banana cream pie.

In order to enjoy the high of being a successful indirect influencer, however, you need to detach yourself as a leader from belief in, and reliance on, the macho image—of the military hero, or the take-no-prisoners guy, or the kick-butt quarterback. Better to go after that image, if you need it, from places and people other than your company and your employees—join the Army Reserve, play poker for big stakes, or play touch football with ex-NFL players every Sunday.

Women generally don't experience the need to emulate that same testosterone-driven likeness. Although they may not necessarily be better at using the Beyond Assertiveness approach than men, they are more likely to view collaborative, rather than competitive, leadership as a value. Many of the new female leaders have chosen a more indirect approach because they view leadership as skill in influencing colleagues and coworkers to participate together as a team to accomplish meaningful goals. A leader has to be able to inspire others to take action, by her actions. This definition tends to fit Beyond Assertiveness better than Command and Control does.

The current governor of Arizona, Jane Dee Hull, is a good example of the kind of leadership I have described. She has said in more than one way and in more than one context: "I want to unite people, to bring them together, not divide them." To bring people together, rather than setting them at odds, often requires skill at indirect influence.

A story about the governor's influencing of the senate majority leader demonstrates her philosophy in action. She apparently hadn't liked some of his public criticism of her handling of the budget process and dropped in unexpectedly at the majority leader's office. Rather than publicly or aggressively telling him to cut it out she met with him quietly and privately, using a collaborative rather than a competitive approach—an indirect rather than direct influence attempt. The governor said, the day after the meeting, in an interview, "I was disappointed that his comments have been directed on a personal level." (Long pause) "But I don't think that's going to happen again." The senate majority leader was immediately and publicly penitent. "I'm quick to apologize to the governor for anything I said that's been construed as personal," he said. "Our communication has not been as good as it should be, so I need to talk directly to her in the future. So we're going to do better, and I'm going to be a little more temperate."

My belief is that the governor would not have produced that same kind of response had she not been indirect. If she had been direct, assertive, or aggressive, if she had butted heads with the senate majority leader, the result would have been hostility and resistance rather than what appears to be a conciliatory and unifying response.

As you begin to try out some of the techniques I've explained in this book, you'll find that you're often using many of them at the same time. You might be Modeling on a full-time basis, but intermittently using Reframing, Humor, and Storytelling together. Or you may find that certain techniques work best for you with certain people and situations and you develop a pattern of using Storytelling with one group, and Confusing with another. Maybe you only use indirect influence to soften a direct influence approach—for example, using the Columbo approach before you tell someone they're not doing an adequate job. Maybe you only use indirect influence once a year, or when you're speaking to large groups, or when you're talking to your business partner. However you choose to fit it into your repertoire, I think you'll find it will add effectiveness to your role as a leader. It will help you to get people to do what you want them to do.

Skill in indirect influence is the difference between inexperienced and mature leadership, between intermediate and advanced communication, between forcefully pushing and gently pulling, between in your face and at your side, between stressful and subtle. And it works to get you what you want as a leader.

You can also be pleasantly amused by the simplicity and ease with which an indirect influence approach can bring around an ardently oppositional person or group. Generally when we try a direct approach first with people who are defensive or resistant, we get very frustrated, angry, and stressed out. When we try an indirect approach first, particularly in a new situation, but with a resistant group, we can achieve the desired outcome painlessly, for ourselves and for the group. You can even find yourself laughing out loud, not at the group members, but at the fun and funny way you circumvented giant obstacles. You can feel like David, knocking out Goliath with a puny slingshot. Like many athletic skills, such as skiing, golfing, or tennis, influencing the right way is easier than doing it the wrong way. And influencing the indirect way is often smoother, simpler, less stressful, and more suave than influencing the direct way.

When you're driving in the snow and your car skids, you can grab hard onto the wheel and attempt to quickly and forcefully correct for the skid. Or you can let the wheel slip through your hands, guiding it slowly and firmly, as a way to go with the skid and stay safe. Let go and get in control rather than grabbing on and forcing it. Sometimes, letting go works best.

Note

1. K. Freiberg, J. Freiberg, and T. Peters, *Nuts! Southwest Airlines' Crazy Recipe for Business and Personal Success* (New York: Bantam Doubleday Dell, 1998).

Appendix

Worksheet

Demonstration, Using Laurel as Influencer

1. *What do I want, from whom?*
   Laurel wants additional work, as an external consultant, from Jack.

2. *What resources of power do I have, in regard to the person I'm trying to influence?*
   Possibly Laurel has reward power—the ability to boost Jack's ego and flatter him, sincerely. But overall, she has less power than he, at least in this influence interaction.

3. *What motive base of power does he or she have?*
   Jack has many resources of power. He has reward power—he can give or not give Laurel work. He has legitimate power as the decision maker for hiring external consultants. He also has expert power. He has been in the field longer than Laurel. He has more power than she does. Guessing about what he might want and need from Laurel, his needs could be: her insights about his team, her approval

of him as a manager, her positive feedback about him as a leader.

4. *Is there a potential match or fit?*
   Yes.

5. *What characteristics do I know about him or her that are relevant to this influence situation?*
   Jack is fairly authoritarian and egocentric, as well as somewhat critical and hard to please. He generally thinks he knows what's best and that he's right about most issues in his field.

6. *What characteristics do I know about myself that are particularly important in this influence situation?*
   Laurel tends to be very assertive and to be annoyed by authoritarian, egocentric people. She tends to prefer directness and can be too blunt at times.

Bibliography

Alberti, R., and M. Emmons. *Your Perfect Right: A Guide to Assertive Living*, 7th ed. San Luis Obispo, CA: Impact Publishers, 1995.

Alessandra, A., and M. O'Connor. *The Platinum Rule*. New York: Warner Books, 1996.

Armstrong, D. *Managing by Storying Around*. New York: Doubleday and Co., 1992.

Bandler, R., and J. Grinder. *Frogs into Princes*. Moab, UT: Real People Press, 1979.

Bandler, R., and J. Grinder. *ReFraming*. Moab, UT: Real People Press, 1982.

Basic Behavioral Science Task Force of the National Advisory Mental Health Council. "Social Influence and Social Cognition." *The American Psychologist*, May 1996, pp. 478–484.

Blanchard, K., and S. Johnson. *The One Minute Manager*. New York: William Morrow and Co., 1982.

Boeck, G. "God, Family and Friends." *USA Today*, June 16, 1999, p. 2C.

Bramson, R. *Coping with Difficult People*. Garden City, NY: Anchor Press/Doubleday, 1981.

Burns, D. D. "Persuasion: The All-Hits, No-Misses Way to Get What You Want." *Self,* April 1981, pp. 67–71.

Canary, D., and K. Dindia. *Sex Differences and Similarities in Communication.* Mahwah, NJ: Laurence Erlbaum Associates Publishers, 1998.

Carli, L. "Gender, Language, and Influence," *Journal of Personality and Social Psychology* 59:11 (1990), pp. 941–951.

Carli, L., S. La Fleur, and C. Loeber. "Nonverbal Behavior, Gender, and Influence." *Journal of Personality and Social Psychology* 68:6 (1995), pp. 1030–1041.

Cartwright, D., and A. Zander, eds. *Group Dynamics: Research and Theory.* New York: Harper and Row, 1968.

Chan-Herur, K. C., and C. Evans. "Dealing Effectively with Cross-Cultural Issues in Influence and Negotiation." Berkeley, Ca.: Barnes and Conti Associates, Inc., 1994.

Cialdini, R. *Influence.* New York: Quill, 1984.

Cirillo, L., and C. Crider. "Distinctive Therapeutic Uses of Metaphor." *Psychotherapy* 32:4 (Winter 1995), pp. 511–519.

Cook, M. "Non-Traditional Jobs for Women." Presentation to AWEE Students, Apr. 6, 1999, Phoenix, Az.

Dodenhoff, J. T. "Intepersonal Attraction and Direct-Indirect Supervisor Influence as Predictors of Counselor-Trainee Effectiveness." Doctoral dissertation, Arizona State University, May 1978.

Dupree, D. "Lakers Can Expect Big Changes," *USA Today,* June 17, 1999, p. 1C.

Elgin, S. *The Last Word on the Gentle Art of Verbal Self-Defense.* New York: Prentice Hall, 1987.

Ellis, A., and R. Harper. *A Guide to Rational Living.* Hollywood, Ca.: Wilshire Books, 1997.

Engel, H. "Spice It Up with Figures of Speech." *The Toastmaster*, February 1999, p. 23.

Ensman, R. "Discussion, Debate and Argument: Getting the Upper Hand." *The Toastmaster*, May 1997, pp. 4–15.

Fournies, F. *Why Employees Don't Do What They're Supposed to Do and What to Do About It*. New York: Liberty Hall Press, 1988.

Gans, J. "The Leader's Use of Indirect Communication in Group Therapy." *International Journal of Group Therapy* 46:2 (1996), pp. 209–228.

Gardenswartz, L., and A. Rowe. "Giving Feedback in a Diverse Environment." *Managing Diversity Newsletter* 6:12 (September 1997), pp. 1, 4.

Gardner, H. *Leading Minds*. New York: Basic Books, 1995.

Goleman. D. *Emotional Intelligence*. New York: Bantam Books, 1997.

Goodman, J. "The Worth of Mirth." *The Toastmaster*, March 1993, pp. 24–26.

Grote, D. "Dealing with Miscreants, Snivelers, and Adversaries." *Training and Development*, October 1998, pp. 19 20.

Haley, J. *Problem-Solving Therapy*. New York: Harper and Row, 1978.

Haley, J. *The Psychiatric Techniques of Milton H. Erickson, M.D. Uncommon Therapy*. New York: W. W. Norton and Co., 1973.

Hall, J. A. *Nonverbal Sex Differences*. Baltimore: The John Hopkins University Press, 1984.

Johnson, K. *Sales Magic* (audiotape). Chicago: Nightingale Conant, 1990.

Jordan, J., and M. Roloff. "Acquiring Assistance from Others: The Effect of Indirect Requests and Relational Intimacy on

Verbal Compliance." *Human Communication Research* 6:4 (Summer 1990), pp. 519–555.

Josefowitz, N. *Paths to Power*. Reading, MA: Addison-Wesley, 1980.

Jung Chan. *Wild Swans: Three Daughters of China*. New York: Doubleday, 1991.

Kaye, B., and B. Jacobson. "True Tales and Tall Tales: The Power of Organizational Storytelling." *Training and Development*, March 1999, pp. 44–50.

Korobkin, D. "Humor in the Classroom: Considerations and Strategies." *College Teaching* 36:4 (Fall 1988), pp. 154–158.

Krakauer, J. *Into Thin Air*. New York: Anchor Books/Doubleday, 1997.

Lloyd, S. *Developing Positive Assertiveness*. Los Altos, Ca.: Crisp Publications, 1988.

Marek, E. *Eating Roses: Bites of Living Humor*. San Jose, Ca.: Decipher Press, 1998.

McClelland, D., and D. Burnham. "Power Is the Great Motivator." *Harvard Business Review*, January–February 1995, pp. 126–139.

McGuire, P. "Therapists See New Sense in Use of Humor." *APA Monitor* 30:3 (March 1999), pp. 1, 10.

Mehrabian, A. *Nonverbal Communication*. Chicago: Aldine Atherton Inc., 1972.

Meichenbaum, D. Telephone interview, October 8, 1997.

Meichenbaum, D., and D. Turk. *Facilitating Treatment Adherence*. New York: Plenum Press, 1987.

Nair, K. "Leadership as Service." Speech presented to the Valley of the Sun chapter of the American Society for Training and Development, Phoenix, Az., May 7, 1999.

Neimeyer, R. "Meaning Reconstruction and the Experience of Loss." Workshop, Mesa, Az., March 19, 1999.

Orben, R. "Why Humor?" *The Toastmaster*, March 1993, pp. 6–7.

Peters, T. Review of David Armstrong's *Managing by Storying Around*. Amazon.com, July 1999.

Price, R. *A Palpable God*. New York: Atheneum, 1978.

Rosen, S. *My Voice Will Go with You: The Teaching Tales of Milton Erickson*. New York: W. W. Norton and Company, 1982.

Rosenblatt, R. "Rules for Aging." *Modern Maturity*, May–June 1999, p. 22.

Shay, J. J. " 'OK, I'm Here, but I'm Not Talking!': Psychotherapy with the Reluctant Male," *Psychotherapy* 33:3 (Fall 1996), pp. 503–513.

Simons, G. "The Uses and Abuses of Humor in a Multicultural World." *Managing Diversity* 7:1 (October 1997), pp. 1, 3.

Sindelar, S. "President's Minute Message." *The Arizona Speaker*, January 1999, p. 2.

Smith. M. J. *When I Say No, I Feel Guilty*. New York: Bantam Books, 1975.

Sobczak, A. "How to Sell with Sizzle Stories." *Sell!ng*, November 1998, p. 12.

Steil, J., and J. Hillman. "The Perceived Value of Direct and Indirect Influence Strategies: A Cross-Cultural Comparison." *Psychology of Women Quarterly* 17:2 (1993), pp. 457–462.

Tingley, J. *Genderflex™: Men and Women Speaking Each Other's Language at Work*. New York: AMACOM, 1994.

Tingley, J. *Say What You Mean, Get What You Want*. New York: AMACOM, 1996.

Trompenaars, F. *Riding the Waves of Culture.* London: The Economist Books Ltd., 1993.

Ward, J. "Try to Tell a Story." *The Toastmaster*, February 1999, pp. 12–13.

Wiley, K. W. "How Southern Belles Outsmart City Slickers." *Savvy*, July 1985, pp. 48–52.

Zemke, R. "Humor in Training: Laugh and the World Learns with You—Maybe." *Training*, August 1991, pp. 26–29.

Index